Understanding Drug Issues

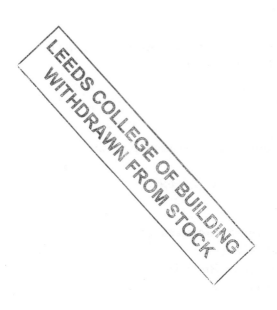

companion volume

Understanding Street Drugs
A Handbook of Substance Misuse for Parents, Teachers and Other Professionals
Second Edition
David Emmett and Graeme Nice
ISBN 1 84310 351 6

of related interest

Listening to Young People in School, Youth Work and Counselling
Nick Luxmoore
ISBN 1 85302 909 2

Supporting Parents of Teenagers
A Handbook for Professionals
Edited by John Coleman and Debi Roker
ISBN 1 85302 944 0

Understanding and Supporting Children with Emotional
and Behavioural Difficulties
Edited by Paul Cooper
ISBN 1 85302 665 4

Adolescence
Assessing and Promoting Resilience in Vulnerable Children
Brigid Daniel and Sally Wassell
ISBN 1 84310 019 3

Helping Adolescents and Adults to Build Self-Esteem
A Photocopiable Resource Book
Deborah Plummer
ISBN 1 84310 185 8

Just Schools
A Whole School Approach to Restorative Justice
Belinda Hopkins
Foreword and Introduction by Guy Masters
ISBN 1 84310 132 7

Deliberate Self-Harm in Adolescence
Claudine Fox and Keith Hawton
Child and Adolescent Mental Health Series
ISBN 1 84310 237 4 pb

Understanding Drug Issues

A Photocopiable Resource Workbook

Second Edition

David Emmett and Graeme Nice

Jessica Kingsley Publishers
London and Philadelphia

First published in 2005
by Jessica Kingsley Publishers
116 Pentonville Road
London N1 9JB, UK
and
400 Market Street, Suite 400
Philadelphia, PA 19106, USA

www.jkp.com

Library of Congress Cataloging in Publication Data
A CIP catalog record for this book is available from the Library of Congress

ISBN-13: 978 1 84310 350 9
ISBN-10: 1 84310 350 8

Printed and Bound in Great Britain by
Athenaeum Press, Gateshead, Tyne and Wear

*With special thanks to Jean Emmett
and the late Alan 'Deano' Dent,
to whose memory this book is dedicated.*

Contents

Introduction

The two of us have been heavily involved in presenting drugs education to young people over many years, and when doing so make it clear that we are not there to tell them 'Don't take drugs'. We would rather that they stayed away from street drugs, for our experience has taught us that, for many of them, not to do so would be a grave mistake. However, it is not for us to tell young people what to think or what to decide. It is for each young person to do that for him- or herself. Furthermore, if we were to simply tell young people not to do a certain thing, and they chose to do it anyway, then the only thing they would have to reject is us. If, on the other hand, we enable them to gain knowledge and greater understanding of many of the issues concerning drug use, then they have to reject all of that knowledge and understanding if they still want to get involved with drugs; a much more difficult task.

Over the past 20 or so years the style of drugs education presented to our young people has gone through many changes. Our early attempts at drug misuse prevention education depended very largely on the principle of 'shock horror'. Films were produced showing dead and dying drug 'addicts', festering injection sites and even shots of the post-mortem examination of dead users. The simple idea was that scenes of such horror could not fail to put young people off taking drugs, and that is how we would have solved the problem. It soon became clear that this approach was failing, and its effects were very short-lived. Young people were indeed shocked and horrified but they were also fascinated. The many research projects carried out at the time showed that at best the approach's deterrent effects did not last, and that in some cases it actually encouraged experimentation. This is perhaps not surprising as most young people believe that they are immortal and that such awful things will not happen to them.

Drug prevention education then moved to the information model. The simple idea was that if teachers taught young people all about drugs, then they would be able to make the right decisions. The flaw in this approach was that, although we gave them all the facts necessary to make a decision, we failed to teach them how to handle the decision-making process itself. Efforts were then made to deal with this flaw by adopting the 'just say no' approach. Fiercely negative messages were added to the facts so that young people were left only with accepting the 'just say no' message or rejecting all that they had been taught.

Clearly, with the rapid escalation in young people's drug use over the last two decades, this approach has also failed to a large extent.

New strategies must therefore be found and utilised whereby young people themselves can be involved in their own education and their views sought and valued. They should be given credit for their own intelligence and insight, and the power that they hold as potential influencers of their peers.

In this workbook the exercises have been devised not to put young people down by telling them that they are wrong, bad or stupid if they use drugs, but to challenge and inform them. The exercises allow participants to explore their knowledge, attitudes and beliefs about today's drug culture, encouraging them to look at the subject in a less insular manner and to consider a whole range of possibilities. They will be able to reason and decide for themselves how they feel about the many issues raised.

In this way these exercises may encourage young people to make informed judgements and decisions about where they fit in around drug use. It is our hope that, by treating them in a responsible, respectful and more adult way, they may then make better-informed decisions as to their own actions, and by doing so may both reduce the level of drug use and also the degree of harm that such use is causing.

The exercises in this workbook take account of many learning styles, and for that matter teaching styles too, and, we hope this will cater for the majority rather than the few. It is our hope that these exercises will stimulate young people and, through raising their awareness, reduce the numbers of those who may go on to experiment with substances and of those who may go on to develop greater problems through prolonged usage.

Exercise 1

What If?

Suggested age: 13+ • Suggested length of exercise: 1 hour

Outline

This exercise allows participants to accept responsibility for preparing advice to the Government which is considering legalising the supply and use of drugs. Participants will have an opportunity to consider the advantages and disadvantages of such action.

Purpose and expected outcome

- To increase awareness of how drugs affect society.
- To increase the participants' sense of community responsibility.
- To encourage individual responsibility over drug decisions.
- To see personal drug use in a wider context.
- To challenge attitudes to drug use.
- To reinforce drug prevention messages.

Method

The teacher or group leader is to outline the exercise and then form the participants into small groups. Each group is allocated a worksheet (1.1–1.6) that covers a different area of responsibility. If the class is large, more than one group may be using copies of the same sheet. Allow time for each group to discuss their sheet fully and to make notes of the points raised. At the end of the allocated time, each group is to report back the results of their discussions. Questions may then be asked by the leader or by other members of the class. The leader can then draw together salient issues that have arisen, and then organise a vote to arrive at a majority decision as to whether drug legalisation would be advantageous or detrimental to society.

Notes for teacher or group leader

Participants may raise the issue of the legal use of alcohol, and you may wish to discuss with the class the fact that alcohol and its social use does not compare with most patterns of illegal drug use. Unlike alcohol, the controlled, low-level and social use of most drugs is very difficult to maintain over any length of time. Most of our common illegal drugs of misuse have effects that are more persistent than alcohol. *Excessive* use of alcohol would be a more relevant comparison, and society already goes to great lengths to control such use, such as monitoring the alcohol consumption of drivers with simple breath-sampling devices.

Participants may wish to set special rules for people in certain positions of responsibility, prohibiting them alone from using drugs. This idea should be resisted, for the same rules should apply to all. There are very few people who do not have some responsibilities for others, so if it is permissible for some people to use drugs then it should be permissible for everyone.

Leaders may wish to use the exercise in modified ways, perhaps specifying only certain illegal drugs, or making the participants look at the issues from the standpoint of different members of society.

Follow-up exercises

1. Participants could collect media articles concerning drug-use incidents and evaluating their effect on society.

2. Participants could write an essay covering differing aspects of drug use.

3. Further group discussion of issues raised during the exercise.

1.1 Armed Forces

You are a member of a team responsible to the Government for the operation of its defence forces.

You have been asked to consider the implications of a proposal to legalise the supply and use of drugs.

You might like to include the following in your considerations:

- personnel on front-line duties, including those in charge of weapons, using mind-altering substances

- military discipline

- military security, official secrets and espionage

- military communications

- the safety of nuclear and other weapons

- co-operation and planning with allies

- negotiations

- the safety of personnel, planes, ships, vehicles, etc

- correct treatment of prisoners of war.

Remember: consider all possible outcomes

✓

1.2 Health Care

You are a member of a team responsible to the Government for the provision of health care in your district.

You have been asked to consider the implications of a proposal to legalise the supply and use of drugs.

You might like to include the following in your considerations:

- use of mind-altering substances by hospital staff

- future needs and cost of health-care provision (e.g. patient numbers)

- health issues around injecting drugs

- use of substances by surgical staff

- the physical health of the nation

- the psychiatric health of the nation

- babies born to drug-using parents

- use of drugs by family doctors, district nurses, dentists, etc.

Remember: consider all possible outcomes

1.3 Education

You are a member of a team responsible to the Government for the provision of education in your district.

You have been asked to consider the implications of a proposal to legalise the supply and use of drugs.

You might like to include the following in your considerations:

- the quality of education

- truancy rates of pupils/absenteeism by staff

- achievement levels of pupils who use drugs and their effect on non-drug-using pupils

- school discipline

- education standards/league tables

- academic reputation of the country

- pupil–teacher relations

- safety during practical lessons, physical activities, science experiments and outside visits.

Remember: consider all possible outcomes

✓

1.4 Law and Order – Public Safety

You are a member of a team responsible to the Government for the provision of community safety and security in your district.

You have been asked to consider the implications of a proposal to legalise the supply and use of drugs.

You might like to include the following in your considerations:

- use of mind-altering substances by police officers/firefighters

- police/firefighter response to incidents

- prison discipline and security

- street crime

- justice, e.g. use of drugs by judges, juries, magistrates or witnesses

- organised crime and terrorism

- road safety

- public order

Remember: consider all possible outcomes

1.5 Tourism

You are a member of a team responsible to the Government for the encouragement of tourism.

You have been asked to consider the implications of a proposal to legalise the supply and use of drugs.

You might like to include the following in your considerations:

- tourists who come just to buy and use drugs

- family tourism to the country

- the reputation of the country in the eyes of foreign tourists

- the arrival of foreign dealers to supply drugs

- street safety in major tourism areas

- the reputation of UK citizens visiting other countries

- relationships with other countries where drugs remain illegal and whose citizens visit the UK.

Remember: consider all possible outcomes

1.6 Employment

You are a member of a team responsible to the Government for employment.

You have been asked to consider the implications of a proposal to legalise the supply and use of drugs.

You might like to include the following in your considerations:

- production levels

- workers operating dangerous machinery while they are affected by substances

- levels of absenteeism and sickness in the workforce

- relationships between staff and employers

- the quality of work that needs high levels of accuracy which is carried out by staff using substances

- relationships between drug-using staff and their non-drug-using colleagues

- business and trades union leaders affected by mind-altering substances while making important decisions

Remember: consider all possible outcomes

Exercise 2

What a Bargain!

Suggested age: 12+ • Suggested length of exercise: 1 hour

Outline

This exercise enables participants to explore some of the issues that are associated with buying drugs. Participants will look first at information that they may wish to have before they can make a sensible decision as to whether to purchase a particular car or not. They will then extend that idea to the purchase of illegal drugs, and the information they require before deciding whether to purchase or not. Participants will have an opportunity to assess how important it is to have accurate information when making such purchases, and to express their views regarding doing so without such information.

Purpose and expected outcome

- To improve participants' understanding of drugs.

- To encourage participants to explore drug-related decisions.

- To challenge attitudes to drug use.

- To reinforce drug prevention messages.

Method

The teacher or group leader is to outline the exercise and then form the participants into small groups. Each group is to be issued with the blank worksheet (2.1) that deals with the purchase of a car. The leader will explain that the participants are to imagine that they have seen a secondhand car and are considering buying it. Each group is then asked to list the information that they need before making up their minds whether to buy or not. Time is allowed for group discussion, and each group reports back to the rest of the class on the issues that they have discussed. The leader may need to restrict feedback, so that every group has a chance to contribute. The answer sheet for 2.1 can then be used as an OHP slide and compared with the ideas raised by the participants. The various categories of information can then be discussed and placed in order of importance.

The blank worksheet (2.2) that deals with the purchase of an illegal drug is then issued, and each group asked to discuss the information they require before deciding whether to purchase or not. Time is allowed for discussion and then each group reports back to the rest of the class on the issues that they have raised. The leader can then use the answer sheet for 2.2 as an OHP slide and compare it with the groups' lists. As with the car purchase, the categories can be discussed and the information placed in order of importance. The class may then be asked to consider where good accurate information can be obtained on both cars and illegal drugs, and the opinion they would hold of somebody who bought a car without previously finding out as much as possible about it. This can then be compared with the way in which most people buy illegal drugs.

Notes for teacher or group leader

The availability of good, balanced and accurate information regarding drugs is very important. Some users or potential users may consider that much of the information that is made available from official sources to be propaganda rather than fact. The leader may obtain supplies of such drugs literature and compare it with information that is available from other bodies working in the drugs field (see Appendix for a list of such bodies).

Follow-up exercises

1. Participants can also collect copies of advertisements for different products and study the information given. They can then assess the degree of importance that manufacturers attach to information they feel purchasers want. A comparison can then be made with the degree of information offered to users by those selling illegal drugs.

2. A further comparison can be made by collecting information that is supplied with medical drugs.

2.1 What Should You Ask Before Buying a Car?

Suggested Answers for Worksheet 2.1

Price & running costs
1. Sale price
2. Affordability
3. Will it hold its value?
4. Servicing costs
5. Tyre costs
6. Fuel consumption
7. Insurance
8. Value for money
9. Guarantee/warranty
10. Repair costs

Performance
1. Engine size
2. Speed
3. Acceleration
4. Road-holding

Legality
1. Roadworthy?
2. Insurance/tax
3. Is it Stolen?

Safety
1. Speed
2. Brakes
3. Road-holding
4. Air bags
5. Tyres/steering
6. Body condition/rust
7. Modified?
8. Suitability for use

Image
1. Colour
2. Style
3. Engine size
4. Speed and acceleration
5. Make/age
6. Entertainment system
7. Satellite navigation
8. Condition

History
1. Mileage/users
2. Service history
3. Reputation

2.2 What Should You Ask Before Buying a Drug?

Suggested Answers for Worksheet 2.2

Price and future costs

1. Sale price
2. Habit-forming?
3. Tolerance
4. Withdrawal
5. Side-effects
6. Availability
7. Affordability

Performance

1. Expected effects
2. Fulfils your needs?
3. Strength/tolerance
4. Method of use
5. Reliability
6. Predictability

Legality

1. Penalties for possession, supply etc.
2. Effects of prosecution on education and future prospects

Safety

1. Strength
2. Purity/additives
3. Snideys (false drugs)
4. Tolerance
5. Overdose
6. Withdrawal
7. Side-effects
8. Method of use
9. Reliability
10. Predictability
11. Risks/dangers
12. Unexpected effects

Image

1. Street credibility
2. Fashionable
3. Reputation
4. Method of use

History

1. Accurate information available?
2. Reputation/background
3. Known problems

Exercise 3

Safety Ladder

Suggested age: 14+ • Suggested length of exercise: 1 hour

Outline

This exercise is designed to allow participants to consider the various degrees of danger associated with both medical and illegal drugs, allied to the way in which they are used, the reasons for use, and the environment in which they are used.

Purpose and expected outcome

- To increase awareness of the potential danger involved in certain behaviour.

- To increase the participants' understanding of the possible outcomes of such behaviour.

- To encourage individual responsibility over drug decisions.

- To challenge attitudes to drug use.

- To reinforce drug prevention messages.

Method

The 'safety', 'danger' and 'midway' positioning cards should first be laid out on a floor or other flat surface, allowing sufficient space in between for all of the situation cards.

The situation cards (3.1) should be handed out, one to each participant or pair of participants if they are working in pairs. Alternatively, they can be asked to choose a card at random. Participants should then be asked to consider the possible problems and dangers of the action written on the card, and to place their card in what they consider to be the right position between the safety and danger positioning cards (3.2). Those that are considered the most or least dangerous should be placed closest to the appropriate card. As they place their card, each participant or pair of participants is asked to justify their reasons for positioning the card where they have. Discussion within the whole group may follow and cards may be repositioned as necessary. If space is limited, the safety ladder sheet (3.3) can be used as a handout, and students should be asked to write the number of the situation card in the appropriate position on the ladder. Alternatively, the ladder sheet can be reproduced as an OHP slide and projected onto a white board. The numbers can then be written on the white board in the appropriate positions.

Notes for teacher or group leader

The accompanying notes refer to the numbered cards and will assist the leader in discussing with the group as to the most appropriate position of each card.

Card 1

Possibility of overdose; danger from adulterants; danger from blood-borne infections (HIV, hepatitis etc.); may miss vein and hit artery or nerve; danger of vein collapse; drug has immediate and irreversible effect.

Card 2

More carcinogenic than tobacco alone; may cause drowsiness, hallucinations, lack of co-ordination, menstruation problems in female users, impotency problems in male users; may cause flashbacks if used in a previous LSD user.

Card 3

Danger from asphyxiation; danger from heart failure; danger of an explosion if near naked flame; possibility of inhalation of vomit, collapse, accident and risk of sudden death with no help at hand.

Card 4

Totally safe!

Card 5

Many fake steroids on market; testicles may shrink permanently; in females clitoris may enlarge; use can cause aggression (roid rages); use associated with cancers, liver damage and personality changes.

Card 6

Friend may panic, have bad experience, become involved in an accident, be permanently affected.

Card 7

May collect wrong kind; possible nausea and vomiting; if prepared for use they become a class A drug.

Card 8

Danger from overheating, dehydration; others around may be unaware of subject's drug use and fail to provide appropriate help in case of illness or collapse; may cause psychiatric problems, death.

Card 9

Risk of drowsiness, nausea, confusion, overheating.

Card 10

Depletes blood sugar; leads to overconfidence, suppressed appetite, weight loss, immune system impairment; withdrawal symptoms include panic, anxiety and insomnia; tolerance may develop.

Card 11

Uncertain effects of mixing drugs; taking similar types of drug may cause overdose; cocktail may prove lethal; effect of one may cancel out that of another or cause a new and unpredictable effect.

Card 12

Uncertain effects of mixing drugs; taking drugs with similar properties may cause overdose; cocktail may prove lethal; effect of one may cancel out that of another or cause a new and unpredictable effect.

Card 13

Unknown effect of new drug; may be 'snidey' pseudo drug.

Card 14

Sweet fruity taste masks alcohol content making it possible to drink too much and become drunk; alcohol impairment and poisoning.

Card 15

Unknown content of capsules, which may contain a dangerous substance; if your friends are adversely affected you could be held legally responsible.

Card 16

Seven per cent purity means 93 per cent of impurities and other unknown substances; injecting could lead to vein collapse, abscesses etc.

Card 17

Seventy per cent purity is much higher than normal street strength and could easily lead to overdose and death; 30 per cent of impurities can still cause problems: collapsed veins, abscesses etc.

Card 18

It is possible to overdose on tranquillisers and sleeping tablets; both types can easily become addictive; neither will remove the cause of the stress.

Card 19

Danger of asphyxiation, especially if the bag is placed over your head or over your nose and mouth.

Card 20

Alcohol and cannabis are both depressant drugs and their use together will exacerbate those depressant qualities; risk of drowsiness, loss of co-ordination, slowing of bodily functions, hallucinations; parents could be charged with permitting the smoking of cannabis at home (maximum penalty 14 years).

Card 21

Having a larger quantity of street drugs on you than would seem usual for one individual could lead to a charge of possession with intent to supply, leading to a heavier sentence.

Card 22

Crack cocaine is habituating, leading to increasing use and therefore costing larger sums of money each time due to developing tolerance; full chemical addiction can develop in a short time.

Card 23

Many impurities and adulterants; dangers of injecting, abscesses, dirty 'hits', collapsed veins; it's a class A drug attracting heavy penalties; danger from overdose; risk of HIV/Hepatitis B and C/gonorrhoea if needles or other injecting equipment (filters, spoons or even water) are shared; danger of disposed needles to people and animals.

Card 24

More alcohol readily available; may get carried away in atmosphere.

Card 25

Use of drugs will not cure loneliness and may add to depression, cause other problems such as paranoia, insomnia, anxiety, debt, plus legal problems.

Card 26

Both drugs are powerful depressants and their use together can easily cause overdose and death.

Card 27

Too much paracetamol is toxic to the kidneys and liver, and overuse can cause permanent damage even leading to death in some cases. Tolerance may build up.

Card 28

Unknown effects on new user; effects may vary with the mood of user and their environment; trip could be good or horrendous; danger of lifelong flashbacks; danger of short- or long-term psychiatric problems; it's a class A drug.

Card 29

Throat tissues may swell causing asphyxiation; fumes may ignite if someone is smoking nearby.

Card 30

Uncertain effects of mixing drugs; one drug may cancel the effect of the other; withdrawal symptoms to both drugs may combine; overdose possible if more drugs are taken.

Follow-up exercises

1. Collecting media articles on drug incidents where danger has been caused.
2. Essay covering differing aspects of drug use and the associated dangers.
3. Further group discussion of issues raised during exercise.

3.1 Safety Ladder Cards (1)

1.

Injecting drugs
using a shared needle
and syringe

2.

Smoking cannabis in a
hand-rolled cigarette

3.

Sniffing lighter fuel
alone in an isolated place

4.

Not using any illegal drug or
intoxicating substance

5.

Injecting anabolic steroids to
help build muscle bulk

6.

Putting an LSD trip in a
friend's drink without
him/her knowing

3.1 Safety Ladder Cards (2)

7.

Collecting, preparing and
using magic mushrooms

10.

Taking speed
to give you energy

8.

Using both ecstasy and speed
in a crowded dance club

11.

Taking various drugs
at the same time

9.

Sniffing 'poppers' handed
to you at a party

12.

Using street drugs
while taking medication
prescribed by your doctor

3.1 Safety Ladder Cards (3)

13. Using a 'howling wolf' or a 'grizzly bear' – new drugs on the scene recommended by a dealer	**16.** Injecting a powder drug that is only 7 per cent pure
14. Drinking alcopops at home	**17.** Injecting a powder drug that is 70 per cent pure
15. Selling pink capsules that you found in the street to your friends	**18.** Using tranquillisers and sleeping tablets because you are stressed

3.1 Safety Ladder Cards (4)

19.

Sniffing a volatile substance
from a plastic bag

22.

Smoking crack
cocaine crystals

20.

Using cannabis
in your bedroom at your
parents' house

23.

Injecting
street heroin

21.

Buying street drugs
on behalf of friends
who gave you the money

24.

Drinking alcohol
in a bar

3.1 Safety Ladder Cards (5)

25.

Taking street drugs
because you feel
depressed and lonely

28.

Trying LSD for the
first time to see
if you like it

26.

Using heroin and alcohol
at the same time

29.

Squirting lighter fuel directly
into the mouth and throat

27.

Taking more paracetamol
than is advised on
the bottle

30.

Using both a stimulant
and a depressant drug
at the same time
(e.g. speed and heroin)

3.2 Safety Ladder Positioning Cards (1)

3.2 Safety Ladder Positioning Cards (2)

3.3 Safety–Danger Ladder

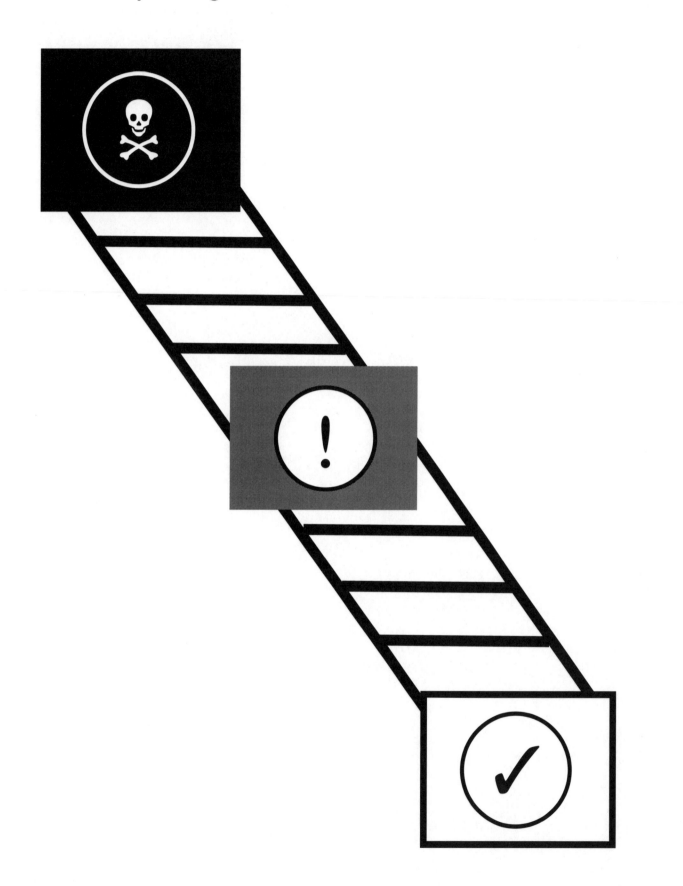

Exercise 4

Slang

Suggested age: 14+ • Suggested length of exercise: 1 hour (+20 minutes for the Wordsearch)

Outline

An exercise that allows participants to improve their knowledge and understanding of drugs and their use, by exploring the subject of drug-related slang.

Purpose and expected outcome

- To improve knowledge and understanding of drugs and their use.
- To demystify drug slang by increasing understanding.
- To deglamourise drug slang by exploring its meaning and origins.
- To challenge attitudes to drug use.
- To reinforce drug prevention messages.

Method

The worksheets (4.1) contain 34 slang words or phrases that are associated with drugs and their use. The sheets can be copied, cut up and laminated for use, or simply used as a source for the teacher or leader to read out to participants. The participants should be divided into groups of four or five, and issued with a number of the slang cards for consideration. If the sheet is being used as a source, then a number of pieces of slang can be read to each group for them to write down. Each group's consideration should include what they understand the word or phrase to mean, and whether there is more than one meaning. The group should also consider where they think the piece of slang originated and how it got its present meaning.

Following sufficient time for discussion, the groups should report back to the rest of the class with their results. The leader can write the slang words on the board together with the meaning and origins that each group has agreed upon. General discussion, exploration of issues raised and further thoughts from the rest of the class should be encouraged and included on the board. When all of the groups have reported back, the leader should draw together the various issues that have been raised and explore with the class whether the pieces of slang present a positive or negative image. The exercise also includes a wordsearch game (4.2) containing 14 pieces of drug slang. This can be used as a short introduction to the subject of slang or as a follow-on activity.

Notes for teacher or group leader

Generally accepted meanings and origins of the slang words and phrases.

Base

Meaning – A potent unadulterated, putty-like form of amphetamine extracted from the manufacturing processes earlier than the usual powder form. Sometimes used to describe smokable cocaine or freebase.
Origins – From its literal meaning: viz, 'the main ingredient of a substance'.

Busted

Meaning – Being searched and/or arrested by the police for drug offences. Also applied to having your house, room or car searched by the police.
Origins – From its literal meaning: viz, 'broken, no longer in working order, bankrupt'.

Cold turkey

Meaning – The process of withdrawing from heroin without medical help; occasionally applied to withdrawal from other drugs.
Origins – During withdrawal from heroin without assistance from prescribed medications the skin of the withdrawer goes through a series of rapid fluctuations in temperature. When the skin is cold it has a clammy feel and is covered in goose pimples. This can give it the appearance of the plucked skin of a dead turkey.

Come-down

Meaning – The feelings of withdrawing from a drug, or simply the feelings experienced as the effects subside.
Origins – From its literal meaning: viz, 'a descent; a disappointment or deflation; a degradation'.

Crack baby

Meaning – The baby born to a mother who has used crack cocaine throughout pregnancy. The baby will be born withdrawing from the drug and in a distressed state, and also is at risk of being born physically or intellectually damaged.
Origins – The word 'crack' is applied to the crystalline form of cocaine because of the noise that the crystals make when they are heated for smoking.

Crash

Meaning – To come down from the effects of a stimulant drug.
Origins – From its literal meaning: viz, 'to fall or rush to destruction and collapse; to fail or fall apart'.

Dealer

Meaning – A dealer in or supplier of drugs, usually for payment.
Origins – From the literal meaning of the word 'deal': viz, 'the act of distributing something'.

Dope

Meaning – Cannabis; occasionally drugs in general.
Origins – From its literal meaning: viz, 'anything supplied to dull, blind or blunt the conscience or insight'; also from its colloquial meaning of a person who is of low intellect, a dullard or a fool.

Downers

Meaning – Any depressant drug, commonly applied to tablet forms of such drugs as tranquillisers.
Origins – From the ability of depressant drugs to lower or slow down the user both emotionally and physically.

Ecstasy

Meaning – A name for MDMA, a hallucinogenic stimulant drug.
Origins – From its literal meaning: viz, 'a state of exalted pleasure or happiness or rapture'.

Euro dollar

Meaning – An ecstasy tablet with a euro symbol imprinted into its surface.
Origins – Most ecstasy tablets have a symbol or simple picture imprinted into their surface. This is done for marketing purposes to imply that different designs give different effects.

Flashback

Meaning – The rerun of a hallucinogenic experience or 'trip' without further use of a drug. Flashbacks are a common feature of LSD use but can also occur with other hallucinogens such as magic mushrooms. They can occur weeks, months or even years after use of the drug has finished.
Origins – From the cinematic technique of showing scenes from a person's past during the course of the narrative.

Hash

Meaning – Short for 'hashish', a name for cannabis resin.
Origins – From the Arabic word 'Hasheesh', which in turn is derived from an Indian dialect word, 'Haschishin', the name for a nineteenth-century group of assassins who made use of the drug.

High

Meaning – The effects felt by a person using a stimulant drug such as amphetamine or cocaine. Sometimes applied to the effects of non-stimulant drugs.
Origins – From the ability of stimulants to lift the user both psychologically and physically.

Hooked

Meaning – To be addicted, either physically or psychologically, to a drug.
Origins – From its literal meaning: viz, 'ensnared upon a hook'. An efficient hook is fitted with a barb to prevent the object that it has ensnared becoming easily unhooked.

Junkie

Meaning – A drug user; more specifically, a person who is addicted to drugs, especially heroin, which is sometimes known as 'junk'.
Origins – Derived from the use of the word in the US as slang for a lunatic; also from the word 'junk' meaning 'worthless rubbish'.

Losing the plot

Meaning – Becoming totally confused or losing all ambition or interest in life, usually as a result of cannabis use. Sometimes applied to a similar effect from the use or withdrawal from other drugs.
Origins – From the literal meaning of the word 'plot': viz, 'the story or scheme of connected events running through a play, novel, etc.'.

Mushies

Meaning – Hallucinogenic or magic mushrooms.
Origins – Simply an altered form of the word 'mushroom'.

Pill

Meaning – An ecstasy tablet; also sometimes called a 'bean'
Origins – From its literal meaning: viz, 'small medicinal tablet'.

Resin

Meaning – Applied to a solid form of cannabis.
Origins – From its literal meaning: viz, 'a substance derived from the sap of a plant'.

Rocks

Meaning – A potent form of smokable cocaine; also known as freebase or crack.

Origins – From its appearance as raison sized lumps.

Roid rage

Meaning – A sudden fit of uncontrollable aggression as a side-effect of using anabolic steroids. These outbursts of aggression can often have sexual overtones and lead to the user committing violent sexual crimes.

Rush

Meaning – The onset of effects from drug use, usually stimulants; also applied to the rapid effect from injecting drugs.

Origins – From its literal meaning: viz, 'to move forward with haste, impetuosity or rashness' or 'to force out of place; to hasten or hustle forward'.

Skunk

Meaning – A form of cannabis produced by cross-breeding different strains of the cannabis plant to produce high levels of the active ingredient delta 9 tetrahydrocannabinol. This variety was first produced in the Netherlands and is also called 'Nederweed'.

Origins – From the unpleasant smell that is produced when it is smoked, said to resemble the pungent spray used by the skunk as a form of defence.

Snidey

Meaning – Something that is sold under the pretence that it is a particular drug, but is actually something else. It is often applied to tablets sold falsely as ecstasy.

Origins – From the literal meaning of the word 'snide': viz, 'sham; counterfeit; base; mean; dishonest; derogatory in an insinuating way; showing malice'.

Special K

Meaning – Ketamine, an anaesthetic and tranquilliser that can induce out-of-body experiences. Sometimes known as Vitamin K.

Origins – From the breakfast cereal of the same name.

Speed

Meaning – Amphetamine sulphate.

Origins – From the stimulation that the user experiences, causing a speeding up of the body's metabolism; also from its literal meaning: viz, to drive at high, or at dangerously, unduly or illegally high, speed.

Speed freak

Meaning – A habituated user of amphetamine.

Origins – 'Speed' is the drug slang for amphetamine. The second part of the phrase comes from the literal meaning of the word 'freak': viz, 'a monstrosity; an eccentric; a weirdly unconventional person; a person who is wildly enthusiastic about something'.

Tab

Meaning – A small square of paper impregnated with the drug LSD, and with a pictogram printed upon it. May also be short for 'tablet'.
Origins – From its literal meaning: viz, 'a small label'.

Track marks

Meaning – The scars left on the skin surface by injecting drugs.
Origins – From the literal meaning of the word 'track': viz, 'a mark or trail left or a sequence or course of actions'.

Trips

Meaning – Small squares of paper impregnated with the hallucinogenic drug LSD, and with pictograms printed upon them.
Origins – From its literal meaning: viz, 'to make a journey'.

Uppers

Meaning – Any stimulant drug, particularly one in tablet form.
Origins – From the ability of stimulants to lift the user both psychologically and physically.

Wacky baccy

Meaning – A name applied to herbal cannabis.
Origins – From the word 'wacky' meaning 'crazy or zany', together with 'baccy', short for tobacco.
Origins – An example of alliteration applied to drug slang. 'Roid' is a shortened version of 'steroid'.

Works

Meaning – The paraphernalia of drug injecting; usually restricted to needles and syringes but can include such items as mixing spoons.
Origins – From it's literal meaning: viz, 'the mechanism to make something operate'.

Follow-up exercises

1. Participants might collect other examples of slang words that apply to things other than drugs.

2. The wordsearch sheet can also be used.

4.1 Slang Cards (1)

4.1 Slang Cards (2)

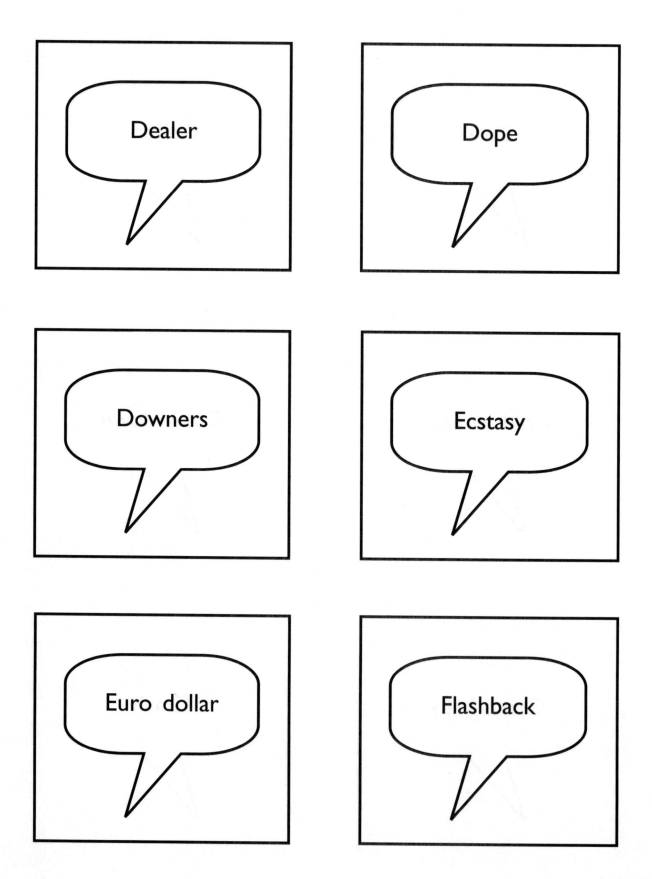

4.1 Slang Cards (3)

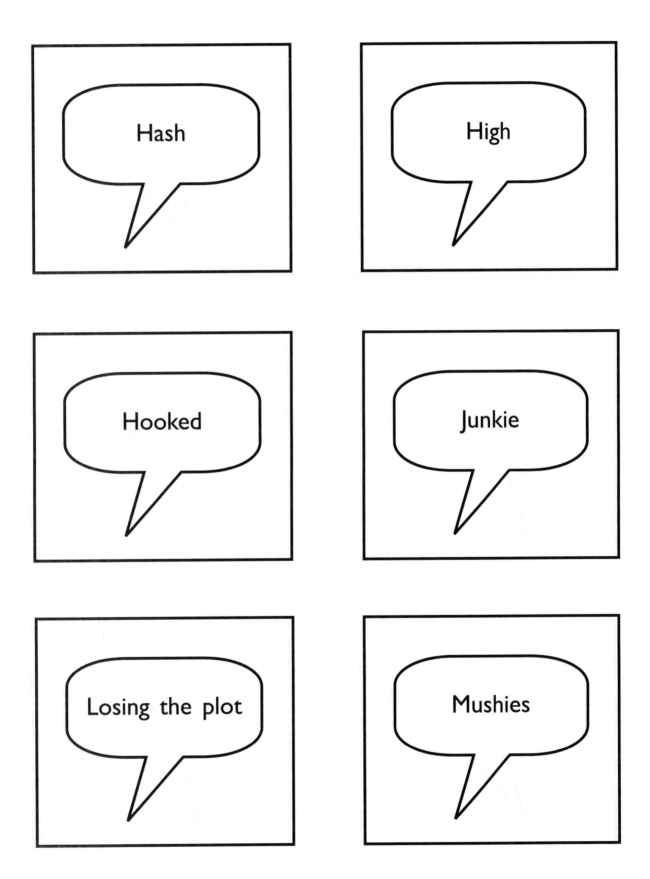

4.1 Slang Cards (4)

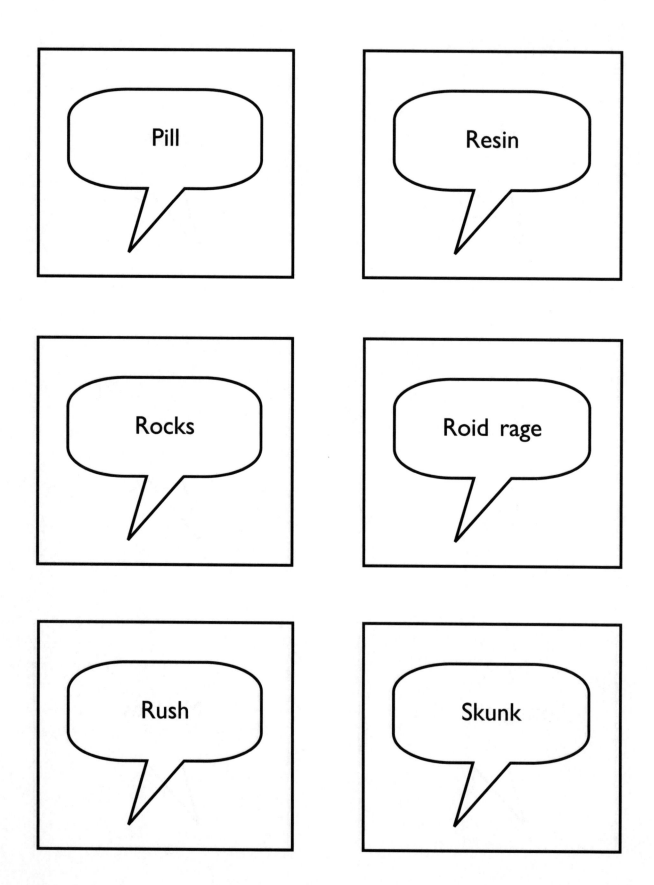

4.1 Slang Cards (5)

4.1 Slang Cards (6)

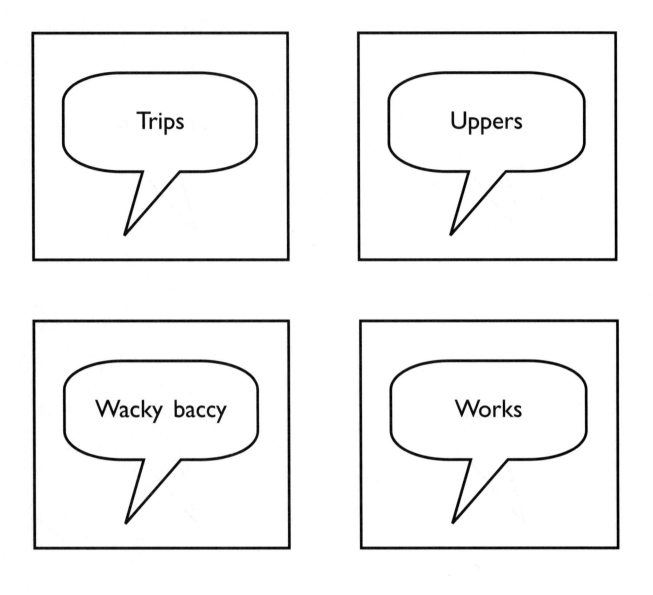

4.2 Wordsearch

The grid contains 14 examples of drug slang. They can be found horizontally, vertically or diagonally and read forwards or backwards.

F	G	M	E	L	S	D	O	W	N	E	R	S	S
J	D	D	F	A	U	P	O	W	L	S	S	C	T
N	W	O	D	E	M	O	C	A	H	W	A	H	A
G	U	P	T	R	I	P	S	C	L	F	A	E	B
A	O	E	T	N	I	J	S	K	N	U	K	S	R
Y	Y	H	C	I	O	I	I	Y	L	S	M	N	N
E	U	N	G	S	R	I	D	B	D	S	A	I	F
K	E	E	Y	Q	T	I	E	A	D	M	V	D	E
R	U	G	I	T	O	A	T	C	X	Z	I	E	L
U	S	A	J	P	Y	H	S	C	R	W	Q	Y	D
T	K	R	E	S	C	C	U	Y	I	A	P	O	O
D	U	D	M	V	D	E	B	F	S	K	S	S	W
L	T	I	W	J	I	D	L	V	R	B	T	H	L
O	L	O	S	I	N	G	T	H	E	P	L	O	T
C	H	R	R	B	A	E	K	O	N	G	D	A	Q

Answers to Worksheet 4.2

F	G	M	E	L	S	D	O	W	N	E	R	S	S
J	D	D	F	A	U	P	O	W	L	S	S	C	T
N	W	O	D	E	M	O	C	A	H	W	A	H	A
G	U	P	T	R	I	P	S	C	L	F	A	E	B
A	O	E	T	E	I	J	S	K	N	U	K	S	R
Y	Y	H	C	H	O	I	I	Y	L	S	M	N	N
E	U	N	G	S	R	I	D	B	D	S	A	I	F
K	E	E	Y	U	T	I	E	A	D	M	V	D	E
R	U	G	I	P	O	A	T	C	X	Z	I	E	L
U	S	A	J	P	Y	H	S	C	R	W	Q	Y	D
T	K	R	E	S	C	C	U	Y	I	A	P	O	O
D	U	D	M	V	D	E	B	F	S	K	S	S	W
L	T	I	W	J	I	D	L	V	R	B	T	H	L
O	L	O	S	I	N	G	T	H	E	P	L	O	T
C	H	R	R	B	A	E	K	O	N	G	D	A	Q

BUSTED   DOPE   ROID RAGE   TRIPS

COME-DOWN   DOWNERS   SKUNK   WACKY BACCY

CRASH   ECSTASY   SNIDEY

COLD TURKEY   LOSING THE PLOT   TAB

Exercise 5

Check It Out

Suggested age: 14+ • Suggested length of exercise: 1 hour

Outline

A quiz in 'true or false' format, designed to allow participants to check out their knowledge of drugs and drug use.

Purpose and expected outcome

- To provide accurate information about drugs and drug use.

- To balance the very largely pro-drug slant of most 'street' information.

- To encourage individual responsibility over drug decisions.

- To challenge attitudes to drug use.

- To reinforce drug prevention messages.

Method

The quiz sheets (5.1) contain 35 questions designed to be suitable for young people aged 14 years and above. They all require answers of either 'true' or 'false'. The teacher or leader can decide on the length of the quiz to suit the time available.

It should be explained to the participants that the purpose of the quiz is not to examine their level of knowledge about drugs and drug use but, rather, to enable them to check out the accuracy or otherwise of the knowledge that they already have, and to add useful and balanced information.

The quiz sheets should be copied and handed out to the participants, and time allowed for them to answer the questions. The teacher or leader should then go through the answers using the guidance notes below. Many of the questions will prompt discussion of associated drug issues. This is intended, and should be encouraged.

Participants should be asked to correct their sheets in line with the given answers and keep them for future reference.

Notes for teacher or group leader

Suggested answers

1. (a) **True**. Put simply – the bigger you are then the more of a particular drug you will need for a particular effect. A person with a large body mass will have a greater quantity of blood to dilute the drug and also a greater number of cells to spread the drug across. One exception to this is LSD; with this drug, the most powerful hallucinogenic substance known, there does not seem to be a close link between required dosage and body mass. Different people do react differently to the same size dose of LSD, but this is the result of other more complicated factors to do with mood and brain chemistry rather than simple body weight.

   (b) **True**. The average woman is smaller than the average man. There are also many hormonal differences that mean that women deal with some drugs differently. Hormonal differences, for example, mean that women process many drugs more slowly and so retain them within the body longer than men.

   (c) **True**. The mood of the user when taking the drug will often have a direct effect on the outcome. This effect is particularly noticeable with hallucinogenic drugs, such as LSD or magic mushrooms, but will also be seen in the use of mind- or mood-altering drugs, such as cannabis, alcohol, ecstasy and so on. Drug users will often refer to their mood on using a drug as their 'mind set'. Users who take their drugs in circumstance and company that are safe and secure and in which they feel relaxed and happy will have a good 'mind set' and be more likely to have a pleasant experience than if the circumstances and company are stressful or insecure and in which the user feels under stress, threatened or unhappy. In these circumstances the outcome is more likely to be unpleasant or frightening.

   (d) **True**. The method used to administer the drug will directly influence the effects that are achieved. Injecting the drug into a vein will result in the most profound effects as it introduces the drug directly and all at once into the bloodstream and from there it will reach the brain within a matter of two or three seconds at the most. Smoking a drug is the second quickest method of introducing it into your blood system, providing the method of smoking does not cause the drug to be weakened or even destroyed. Taking a drug by mouth is the slowest method of introducing it into the body and generally will achieve the least profound effects.

   (e) **True**. Previous use of any drug will mean that tolerance will have begun to develop; this is particularly true with regular use. Tolerance means that the user requires more and more of the drug to achieve a certain level of effects as regular use continues.

2. **False**. Addiction or dependence, either physical or psychological, can develop to any drug with regular use by any method.

3. **True**. The effects of withdrawal from heroin use without medical help can be described as being like a bout of the worst flu that you can imagine. This, of

course, only describes the physical symptoms; the psychological cravings for the drug can be extremely powerful. It needs emphasising that the vast majority of addicted heroin users do not recover to become drug free. Addicted users have a less than one in ten chance of a complete recovery.

4. **True**. Tolerance develops to all drugs with regular use. Tolerance means that the user requires more and more of the drug to achieve a certain level of effects as regular use continues.

5. **True**. Withdrawal symptoms can be both physical and psychological. Their intensity will be dependent upon the amount and regularity of alcohol use. Symptoms can range from trembling limbs, lack of concentration and headaches to unbearable cravings and hallucinations (delirium tremens).

6. **False**. Intense intoxication from alcohol takes a relatively long time to develop and a much longer time to pass. A dose of alcohol takes around one hour to be fully absorbed by the body and is cleared from the system at the rate of approximately one unit (10ml absolute alcohol) per hour. Intense intoxication from solvent abuse can come on within a matter of seconds of commencing the use of the solvent. With powerful solvents, such as liquid petroleum gas, intense intoxication will be felt within 20 to 30 seconds. The chemicals are readily taken up by the user's bloodstream but are also rapidly given up. An intoxicated solvent user will return to sobriety within a short time, around 30 minutes on average. This difference in the time taken to go from sober to intoxicated and back again between alcohol and solvents only serves to emphasise the very real differences between the two methods of achieving intoxication.

7. **True**. When most of the substances being sniffed were solvent glues and liquid solvents, the majority of deaths were caused by accidents in which the user became involved due to his or her intoxicated state. With the increase in the misuse of liquid petroleum gas (LPG) and aerosols propelled by LPG, this has changed. The majority of deaths are now due directly to the effects of such products. LPG causes sudden death in two common ways. The extreme cold produced by releasing the pressurised gas directly into the throat causes the throat and larynx tissues to swell, causing asphyxiation. LPG also causes the overproduction of the hormone adrenaline, which can lead to overstimulation of the heart and heart failure.

8. **False**. A commonly held belief that is now very much out of date. Use of cannabis can lead directly to cancers of the mouth, tongue, throat and lungs. Its use can be a causational factor in certain mental illnesses, including schizophrenia and psychosis. It can cause disruption of the menstrual cycle and damage to an unborn foetus. In males it can lead to reduction in testosterone levels and associated impotency problems. Cannabis is as yet little understood and new problems are emerging as its investigation continues.

9. **True**. This is true in the sense that it can damage the normal operation of the brain. Use of LSD can produce powerful hallucinations for the user that can cause deep psychological trauma. Its use can activate latent mental illnesses that

might have remained inactive without its use. Many users also experience 'flashbacks' weeks, months or even years after using LSD. A 'flashback' is a rerun of the trip without further use of the drug.

10. **False**. Ecstasy or MDMA has been the direct cause of a large number of deaths involving young people. The drug can cause sudden death in a number of ways, overheating – leading to convulsions and collapse and strokes caused by the formation of blood clots – being perhaps the most common. Any user also needs to take into account the potential that the use of ecstasy has for activating latent mental illnesses and causing profound changes in personality. Tolerance to the drug quickly builds up, leading to the need for higher and higher doses which increases the chance of an adverse reaction. The drug is noted for its unpredictability and just because someone has experienced previous safe use of it does not mean that any future use will be similarly safe.

11. **True**. Many users experience 'flashbacks' weeks, months or even years after using LSD. A 'flashback' is a rerun of the hallucinogenic trip without further use of the drug. These reruns are usually of shorter duration but can be very distressing. They can occur at any time and often without warning, placing the sufferer, and perhaps those around him or her, in serious danger. Research indicates that a person who uses cannabis in the same time period as he or she uses LSD will have an increased risk of suffering flashbacks.

12. **False**. The act of injecting drugs alone will not infect anyone with HIV. Sharing injecting equipment with anyone who is infected with HIV will place the user at great risk of becoming similarly infected. Injecting equipment includes not only the needle and syringe but also the spoon or other vessel used to prepare the drug for injection. All such equipment can easily become contaminated with infected blood. Free issues of clean needles and syringes are available in almost all areas in order to reduce the risk of this type of infection.

13. **True**. Experiments were carried out in the 1920s and early 1930s in the UK, and in the 1960s in the US, to test the possibility of using ecstasy (MDMA) as a treatment for certain psychiatric illnesses. The drug proved of little benefit and was extremely unpredictable in its side-effects; it has no permitted medical use.

14. **True**. Ecstasy is a class A drug and supply of the same carries a potential maximum penalty on indictment of life imprisonment together with an unlimited fine and the confiscation of any drug-related assets.

15. **True**. Cannabis is a class C drug and possession carries a maximum penalty on indictment of two years' imprisonment and an unlimited fine.

16. **True**. Amphetamine (speed) use carries a very real risk of serious and often permanent damage to psychiatric health. Many users become depressed and anxious after using for only a short time. Longer use can lead to paranoia, delusions and psychosis. Often these illnesses will require inpatient treatment in psychiatric hospitals and can prove difficult if not impossible to cure.

17. **False**. Cannabis contains some 50 per cent more recognised cancer-causing substances than tobacco. Its smoke is much hotter and more tar-laden than tobacco and has a potential for causing cancer that is at least as high if not higher than tobacco.

18. **False.** If figures are examined for the population as a whole the percentage of people who have ever used an illegal drug in their lives drops down into single figures. It is only in the younger generation that the figures become significantly high. The scale of young people's drug use today is a totally new phenomenon. No generation within recorded history has used drugs on this scale before; it is impossible to predict what the outcome is likely to be.

19. **False**. The offence of supplying requires only that an illegal drug is supplied to another person; it does not require the exchange of any money or other thing. A person giving a drug to someone as a gift commits the offence of supplying. Even sharing a cannabis cigarette with someone counts as supplying. Supplying drugs carries the highest penalties of all drug offences.

20. **False**. Possessing fresh and unprocessed magic mushrooms is not an offence under the drug legislation. Any act of preparing them for consumption, such as drying, cooking or chopping, means that they become controlled substances under class A of the Misuse of Drugs Act 1971 (as amended) and attract the same penalties as heroin. Picking wild magic mushrooms, for your own use or for sale, on land that belongs to someone else and without the landowner's permission, can be an offence under the Theft Act 1968.

21. **False**. A person would need a good level of knowledge of fungi to positively identify members of the magic mushroom group when seen growing. When they have been dried it would require the services of a laboratory to correctly identify them. Many of the problems caused by magic mushrooms are the result of a person using the wrong varieties, many of which are highly toxic.

22. **True and false**. This depends upon your gender. In females the clitoris can become very enlarged and painfully sensitive. In males steroid use can cause the genitalia to shrink. These changes can become permanent.

23. **False**. Cannabis use can lead to a powerful psychological dependency. The authors of this quiz have dealt with cannabis users who could not get out of bed in the morning without smoking the drug first; they felt unable to face the world without its use. This use of the drug then continued throughout the day.

24. **False**. Ecstasy is a class A drug like heroin.

25. **False**. Most drugs sold on the streets have been mixed or 'cut' with other substances in order to increase their weight and bulk and therefore the dealers' profit levels. Some of these cutting agents can be harmless, such as milk powder, glucose and vitamin C powder, while others can be very dangerous. Substances such as chalk, talcum powder, brick dust, cleaning agents, fertilisers, rodent poisons or other drugs have frequently been found cut with street drugs. The purity levels of street drugs can vary considerably, making their

effects difficult to predict. Many users have suffered fatal overdoses as a result of buying a drug at an unusually high level of purity.

26. **False**. It would be very dangerous to rely on this. It is true to say that most police forces warn persons arrested in possession of small amounts of drugs for their own personal use, but this is not guaranteed to happen. There will be circumstances in which they will consider a court appearance to be more appropriate. Warnings are increasingly used for a first such offence only; any subsequent arrests will almost certainly lead to a court appearance. If found guilty in court, the user will have acquired a drugs criminal record, and such a record may prove an insurmountable obstacle to many choices of career. The armed forces, the civil service, most local governments and many companies will not employ people with such a record. Many foreign countries will not issue work or residential permits to convicted drug users and some will not even issue a visa to visit on holiday.

27. **True**. The act of injecting brings with it many problems. Using injecting equipment that has been used by other people lays the user open to contracting any infection that the other user may have. Infections such as HIV, Hepatitis B and C, septicaemia and gonorrhoea are commonly passed on in this way. Injecting impure drugs that contain solids can cause blocked veins, leading to vein collapse and gangrene. Injection sites frequently become infected and abscesses are common. The drug is injected directly into the blood system and reaches the central nervous system within seconds. Once injected it cannot be removed and any overdosing is difficult to counter. With drugs taken orally the excess can often be pumped or washed from the stomach.

28. **False**. The withdrawal effects of amphetamine use will vary according to the amount that the user has been taking and the duration and regularity of the use. Most inexperienced users who have only taken a small to moderate amount of amphetamine will experience a period of tiredness and loss of strength. This can be dealt with by allowing the body to rest, sleep being the best way of doing this. If the use of the drug has been at a much higher level or over an extended period, the withdrawal effects will be much more severe. Many such users will find it extremely difficult to cope with the feelings of anxiety, panic, paranoia and insomnia that such withdrawal will bring. Anyone attempting to give up the use of amphetamine after heavy or prolonged use is well advised to seek the advice and guidance of a professional drug service.

29. **True**. It is impossible to overstate the power of heroin. It is very difficult, if not impossible, for most users to prevent themselves becoming addicted, both chemically and psychologically, to the drug. In the UK over 90 per cent of addicted heroin users never succeed in becoming drug free. Every person tempted to try heroin needs to be very clear about this; the 'power of the powder' is likely to be much stronger than they are and once they begin heroin use they are entering a world from which it can be impossible to escape.

30. **True**. Any drug used by a pregnant woman will also enter the bloodstream of the unborn infant. Crack cocaine causes especially severe problems if used by pregnant women. Many of them will suffer spontaneous abortions due to placental displacement. Many babies will be stillborn. The chief cause of these problems is the way in which all forms of cocaine restrict the flow of blood along veins and arteries, which significantly reduces the volume of blood flowing through the umbilical cord into the foetus. This reduction, together with the consequent reduction in oxygen supply, often leads to the baby being born either physically or neurologically damaged, or both. Some of this damage can be extreme. Even if the child is lucky enough to avoid any pre-birth damage it is likely to be born withdrawing from crack use, which will be extremely unpleasant and potentially very dangerous for the child.

31. **True**. The withdrawal effects of many drugs can lead to aggression on the part of the user. This is true of most stimulants and especially true of crack cocaine. The feelings can be very unpleasant and can easily lead to uncontrollable outbursts of aggression. Such outbursts are a regular feature of the use of anabolic steroids. So common are they that they are given a special name, 'roid rages'; these can be spectacular and include a sexual element in the aggression which can lead the user to commit violent sexual crimes.

32. **True**. Using two drugs of a similar nature, such as two stimulants or depressants, can lead to overdose. Mixing drugs of differing natures can lead to unpredictable and often dangerous results.

33. **False**. The dilation of the blood vessels within the body caused by the inhalation of poppers leads to a dramatic reduction in blood pressure. The heartbeat rises in an attempt to maintain adequate blood pressure. Severe dizziness and blackouts together with nausea and vomiting are common. These factors together increase the risk of the user inhaling his or her own vomit and choking to death. There have been reports of strokes and heart attacks following extensive use of poppers in people who may have had some underlying defect to their cardiovascular system. Some users report that their use of poppers leaves them with severe headaches and sore eyes. Poppers can cause a variety of skin problems including dermatitis. Poppers can cause damage to the eyes if it comes into contact with them and the drinking of the product can lead to severe poisoning.

34. **False**. At the time of writing there are no approved medical uses for cannabis. A number of areas of research are currently underway. Cannabis is being investigated as a possible drug for the alleviation of the nauseous effects of chemotherapy, as an appetite stimulant in wasting diseases, to reduce muscle spasm in multiple sclerosis and to reduce eyeball pressure in glaucoma sufferers. All of this research is ongoing and has not yet been concluded. Until it is it would be unsafe to suggest that cannabis should be used medically in such cases. Medical history is littered with examples of drugs that appeared to have a beneficial part to play in combating certain conditions only to cause dangerous problems with unforeseen side-effects. Should cannabis show a

beneficial effect in the treatment of these disorders then it will be made available in a medical form, not in a smoking form. Even if it passes all the drug safety tests this would not mean that it is safe to be used by people who are not suffering from the particular medical conditions it treats. Heroin, amongst others, has a respected place in the medical treatment of certain conditions and such use improves the lives of the sufferers. This does not mean that heroin is safe for others to use.

35. **True**. Between a quarter and a third of all the recorded solvent deaths each year in the UK are of people who have no previous history of solvent use. Solvents have a real potential to cause sudden death the first time that they are used.

Follow-up exercises

The quiz will have raised many issues connected with drug use. Any of these can be followed up with discussions, research projects, essay writing or in any other way that the group leader sees as being appropriate and useful.

5.1 Check It Out (1)

		True	False
1.	Effects of drugs are influenced by:		
	(a) body weight	☐	☐
	(b) gender	☐	☐
	(c) mood	☐	☐
	(d) method of use	☐	☐
	(e) previous use.	☐	☐
2.	Addiction only develops when drugs are injected.	☐	☐
3.	Withdrawal from heroin is similar to a bout of 'flu.	☐	☐
4.	Tolerance can develop to all drugs, including nicotine and alcohol.	☐	☐
5.	There are withdrawal symptoms from alcohol.	☐	☐
6.	Intoxication from sniffing solvents usually lasts for hours.	☐	☐
7.	Most sniffing deaths are caused by the poisonous effects of the substance used.	☐	☐
8.	There is no evidence of long-term harm from cannabis use.	☐	☐
9.	LSD use can cause brain damage.	☐	☐
10.	Ecstasy is a safe drug for recreational use.	☐	☐
11.	Flashbacks are possible after LSD use.	☐	☐
12.	Injecting drugs will give you HIV and AIDS.	☐	☐
13.	Ecstasy has been used medically in psychiatric hospitals.	☐	☐
14.	The maximum penalty for giving one ecstasy tablet to a friend could be life imprisonment.	☐	☐
15.	The maximum penalty for the possession of just one cannabis cigarette could be two years' imprisonment.	☐	☐

5.1 Check It Out (2)

		True	False
16.	Amphetamine can cause personality disorders and mental illness.	☐	☐
17.	Cannabis does not cause cancer.	☐	☐
18.	Most people experiment with drugs at some time in their lives.	☐	☐
19.	You have to sell drugs to others before you can be charged with supplying.	☐	☐
20.	Magic mushrooms are not illegal.	☐	☐
21.	It is easy to tell magic mushrooms from other more poisonous varieties.	☐	☐
22.	Steroid use can enlarge your genitals.	☐	☐
23.	Cannabis is not addictive.	☐	☐
24.	Ecstasy is a class B drug like amphetamine.	☐	☐
25.	Street drugs are generally pure.	☐	☐
26.	The police only issue warnings for possession of drugs these days.	☐	☐
27.	Injecting is the most dangerous way to use any drug.	☐	☐
28.	There are no withdrawal effects from amphetamine use.	☐	☐
29.	If you get addicted to heroin you probably won't get off it.	☐	☐
30.	Pregnant women who use crack are risking their babies' health.	☐	☐
31.	Some drug use can cause aggression.	☐	☐
32.	Mixing drugs is especially dangerous.	☐	☐
33.	There are no ill effects from using poppers.	☐	☐
34.	Cannabis is used medically.	☐	☐
35.	People have died the first time they sniffed solvents.	☐	☐

Exercise 6

Fact or Fiction?

Suggested age: 11+ • Suggested length of exercise: 1 hour

Outline

A quiz in 'true or false' format, designed to allow participants to check out their knowledge of drugs and drug use.

Purpose and expected outcome

- To provide accurate information about drugs and drug use.

- To balance the very largely pro-drug slant of most 'street' information.

- To encourage individual responsibility over drug decisions.

- To challenge attitudes to drug use.

- To reinforce drug prevention messages.

Method

The quiz sheets (6.1) contain 20 questions designed to be suitable for young people aged 11 years and above. They all require answers of either 'true' or 'false'. The teacher or leader can decide on the length of the quiz to suit the time available.

It should be explained to the participants that the purpose of the quiz is not to examine their level of knowledge about drugs and drug use but, rather, to enable them to check out the accuracy or otherwise of the knowledge that they already have and to add useful and balanced information.

The quiz sheets should be copied and handed out to the participants, and time allowed for them to answer the questions. The teacher or leader should then go through the answers using the guidance notes below. Many of the questions will prompt discussion of associated drug issues. This is intended and should be encouraged.

Participants should be asked to correct their sheets in line with the given answers and to keep them for future reference.

Notes for teacher or group leader

Suggested answers

1. **False**. Dope, marijuana, grass and cannabis are all the same drug. All forms contain the same active ingredient, a complex substance called delta 9 tetrahydrocannabinol. There are some 200 names for cannabis in its various forms.

2. **True**. Ecstasy is not produced commercially anywhere in the world and consequently has no established form. It is produced illegally in a bewildering variety of shapes, sizes, forms and colours. It is very easy for users to be sold tablets and capsules as ecstasy that turn out to be other substances. These are known in drug slang as 'snideys', and may include very powerful and dangerous medical products.

3. **True**. Most drugs sold on the streets have been mixed or 'cut' with other substances in order to increase their weight and bulk, and therefore the dealers' profit levels. Some of these cutting agents can be harmless, such as milk powder, glucose and vitamin C powder, while others can be very dangerous. Substances such as chalk, talcum powder, brick dust, cleaning agents, fertilisers and rodent poisons or other drugs have frequently been cut with street drugs. The purity levels of street drugs can vary considerably, making their effects difficult to predict. Many users have suffered fatal overdoses as a result of buying a drug at an unusually high level of purity.

4. **True**. Any user needs to take into account the potential that ecstasy use has for activating latent mental illnesses, such as psychosis and schizophrenia, and for causing profound changes in personality. Tolerance to the drug quickly builds up leading to the need for higher and higher doses which increases the chance of an adverse reaction. The drug is noted for its unpredictability, and previous safe use of it does not mean that any future use will be similarly safe. Ecstasy, or MDMA, has been the direct cause of a large number of deaths involving young people. The drug can cause sudden death in a number of ways; for example, overheating leading to convulsions and collapse, and strokes caused by the formation of blood clots.

5. **False**. Between a quarter and a third of all the recorded solvent deaths each year in the UK are of young people who have no previous history of use. Solvents have a real potential to cause sudden death on first time use. The most common solvent currently being misused is liquid petroleum gas (LPG), found in pressurised canisters for cooking or heating, as a lighter fuel, and as the propellant in most aerosols. These are usually squirted directly into the throat, and can cause sudden death in two ways. The release of the pressure causes a profound drop in temperature, and causes the tissues of the throat and larynx to swell, leading to asphyxiation. LPG can also lead to the overproduction of the hormone adrenaline, which can lead to heart failure.

6. **True**. Using two drugs of a similar nature, such as two stimulants or depressants, can lead to overdose. Mixing drugs of differing natures can lead to unpredictable and often dangerous results.

7. **False**. Generally, males use drugs more commonly and in larger quantities than females. This picture is slowly changing, however, with an increasing number of females taking to drug use. They are still outnumbered by the male users, but are increasing at a faster rate.

8. **True**. Many users report that they become involved in drug use in order to enhance their image with their peers. The image that such use has for some young people is of someone who is 'cool', 'smart', 'hard', 'in fashion' and so on. It needs saying, however, that many other young people view drug use as foolish and 'uncool'. Many drug users will achieve the opposite reaction to the one that they are seeking from their peers.

9. **False**. A person would need a good level of knowledge of fungi to positively identify members of the magic mushroom group when seen fresh. Once they have been dried, it would require the services of a laboratory to correctly identify them. Many of the problems caused by magic mushrooms are the result of a person using the wrong varieties, some of which are highly toxic.

10. **True**. Recent research has shown that young people who smoke tobacco are approximately four times more likely to become involved in taking illegal drugs. The reason is quite simple, for most young people have their first experience of illegal drugs with cannabis in a smoking form. It is much easier to say yes to an offer of cannabis in this form if you are already a smoker of cigarettes. Smokers have to accustom their bodies to accept the act of smoking; therefore they are very unlikely to make their first smoking experience one of using cannabis.

11. **True**. Addiction or dependence, either physical or psychological, can develop to any drug with regular use by any method.

12. **True**. Tolerance develops to all drugs with regular use, meaning that the user requires increasing amounts of the drug to achieve a certain level of effect if regular use continues.

13. **False**. The act of injecting brings with it many problems. Using injecting equipment that has already been used by others exposes the user to any infections that the previous users may have. Infections such as HIV, Hepatitis B and C, septicaemia and gonorrhoea can be contracted in this way. Injecting impure drugs that contain undissolved solids can block small blood vessels, leading to possible vein collapse and gangrene. Injection sites frequently become infected and abscesses are common. If a drug is injected directly into the blood system it reaches the central nervous system within seconds. Once injected it cannot be removed and any overdosing is difficult to counter. With drugs taken orally they can often be pumped or washed from the stomach or vomited spontaneously.

14. **False**. Amphetamine (speed) use carries many physical risks and problems. Amphetamine is a powerful stimulant that leads to an increase in blood pressure, heart rate and body temperature. Any of these can lead to strokes or heart failure. Amphetamine is also a powerful appetite suppressant and disrupter of sleep patterns, and its use can lead to extreme weight loss and chronic insomnia. These two together can lead to a loss of body condition and a reduction in the efficiency of the body's immune system.

   Amphetamine use carries a very real risk of serious and often permanent damage to psychiatric health. Many users become depressed and anxious after using for only a short time. Longer use can lead to paranoia, delusions and psychosis. Often these illnesses will require inpatient treatment in psychiatric hospitals and can prove difficult if not impossible to cure.

15. **True**. No one starts to use illegal drugs in order to have a bad time; everyone starts with the idea that they will have a good time or perhaps that drug use will mask unpleasant things in their lives. It has to be stated, however, that many users find that they have a very bad time indeed. Their entire lives can become totally dominated by their drug use, with dire consequences. A true friend would never encourage anyone to become involved in such a nightmare. It is a sad fact that the vast majority of young people who use drugs are introduced to them, and indeed even supplied, by a close friend. This may be because the friend is also a user and will be keen to get others involved to make themselves feel better about their own use.

16. **True**. This is true in the sense that the possession of illegal drugs is an illegal act and as such makes everyone who uses such drugs a criminal. Drug use is extremely common, indeed almost normal, among people involved in crimes of dishonesty, but such use is not confined to these types of people. It can affect anyone. Drug use is no respecter of race, social background, gender, academic ability or financial position. There is no such person as a typical drug user, for it could be anyone.

17. **True**. Many of the drugs prescribed by doctors have the potential to cause addiction, either physical or psychological. This is particularly true of tranquillisers and sleeping tablets, and there are many thousands of people in the UK who are addicted to such products as a result of unwise prescribing. Doctors are now very aware of the addictive properties of some prescribed drugs and take great care to avoid their patients becoming addicted to them.

18. **True**. The sniffing of solvents will lead to rapid intoxication. Continued use can then lead on to loss of control over the user's bladder and bowels.

19. **False**. Many thousands of people die each year as a direct result of becoming intoxicated with alcohol. Many of these deaths are of young people. A person who is intoxicated can easily become involved in a reckless act that can lead to a serious accident. These accidents can place innocent bystanders in mortal danger as well as the intoxicated person. Besides the risk of accidents intoxicated people can become involved in criminal acts, unsafe sex or simply make complete and deeply embarrassing fools of themselves.

20. (a) **True**. It is easy for a person whose judgement has been affected by their drug use to become involved in unprotected sex. This could easily lead to an unplanned pregnancy or even to a sexually transmitted disease.

    (b) **True**. Many street drugs can be purchased in small quantities at a low price. Once tolerance and addiction have been established, however, drug use can become very expensive. A common way of paying for such drug use is by becoming involved in crime. This will commonly be in the form of either drug dealing or theft, often accompanied by violence. It has been estimated that some 70 per cent of the crime committed in the UK is drug related.

    (c) **True**. Drugs are easily obtained on credit and a considerable debt can quickly be built up. This places the debtors firmly in the control of the drug supplier. They may be required to carry out a whole range of criminal acts to clear off their debts or may be the subject of a great deal of personal violence.

    (d) **True**. In order to finance an established drug habit, some users, both males and females, may turn to prostitution. This places them at grave risk of violence and of becoming infected with HIV or other sexually transmitted diseases.

    (e) **True**. Many schools will enforce a policy of permanent exclusion for any involvement in drugs. This can have a seriously damaging effect on education and long-term career prospects.

Follow-up exercises

The quiz will have raised many issues connected with drug use. Any of these can be followed up with discussions, research projects, essay writing or in any other way that the leader sees as being appropriate and useful.

6.1 Fact or Fiction? (1)

		True	False
1.	Dope, marijuana, grass and cannabis are different drugs.	☐	☐
2.	Medical drugs are often sold to young people as ecstasy.	☐	☐
3.	Street drugs are usually sold mixed with other substances.	☐	☐
4.	Ecstasy can cause mental health problems.	☐	☐
5.	Solvent sniffing has never killed anyone first time.	☐	☐
6.	Mixing different drugs can be especially dangerous.	☐	☐
7.	Girls use drugs more than boys.	☐	☐
8.	Some people use drugs to look tough.	☐	☐
9.	It's easy to identify magic mushrooms from other kinds.	☐	☐
10.	Smoking cigarettes can lead to the use of other drugs.	☐	☐
11.	Regular use of any drug can lead to addiction.	☐	☐
12.	If a drug is used regularly the effect reduces unless the amount is increased.	☐	☐

6.1 Fact or Fiction? (2)

		True	False
13.	Injecting is no more dangerous than any other way of using drugs.	☐	☐
14.	Amphetamine (speed) is a safe drug for recreational use.	☐	☐
15.	A good friend will not encourage you to take drugs.	☐	☐
16.	All people who use illegal drugs are criminals.	☐	☐
17.	Some people become hooked on certain drugs prescribed by doctors.	☐	☐
18.	Solvent use can make you lose control of your bladder.	☐	☐
19.	Getting drunk on alcohol never hurt anyone.	☐	☐

20. Drug use can lead to:

		True	False
(a)	pregnancy	☐	☐
(b)	crime	☐	☐
(c)	debt	☐	☐
(d)	prostitution	☐	☐
(e)	exclusion from school.	☐	☐

Exercise 7

Can You Help Me Please?

Suggested age: 13+ • Suggested length of excercise: 1 to 1.5 hours

Outline

An exercise to place the participants in situations where they are required to respond to others who are appealing for their help in dealing with a drug-related situation.

Purpose and expected outcome

- To encourage participants to consider the difficulties encountered by drug users and others around them who are affected.

- To encourage participants to consider all of the aspects of a drug situation and to look at ways in which those who are adversely affected by it can be helped.

- To discover what resources are available to help people with a drug-related problem.

- To encourage individual responsibility over drug decisions.

- To challenge attitudes to drug use.

- To reinforce drug prevention messages.

Method

The teacher or leader should briefly explain the exercise and then split the class up into groups of four or five. Each group should be given a copy of one of the letters. It may be that with large classes more than one group will have the same letter to work with. Each group is instructed to consider the letter in detail and to prepare an answer that gives, to the best of their ability, advice that will enable the writer to resolve the situation in a positive manner. After sufficient time has elapsed for discussion, each group is asked to report back to the rest of the class the results of their discussions. This report can take the form of reading out a response letter that the group have composed or, more simply, stating the points that they have considered. The rest of the class should be encouraged to ask questions, to challenge any of the advice given, and to offer suggestions of their own.

Notes for teacher or group leader

It is important that the groups consider as many aspects as possible of the problems detailed in the letters and, in particular, how the actions of any one of the characters involved in the situation can affect those around them.

A list of agencies that offer help and advice to people involved in drug-related situations is provided in the Appendix. Participants may like to find out whether there are more locally based services in their area.

Follow-up exercises

1. The letters can be set as an individual exercise with participants giving verbal or written answers. The class can be instructed to carry out research and draw up a list of helplines and agencies in their locality.

2. The class can examine advice columns in newspapers and magazines, particularly those aimed at young readers, and discuss the level and quality of advice given.

7.1 Richard's Letter

Meadowlands
Orchard Lane
Tynesworth

Dear Lisa

I am 13, my parents are divorced and I live with my mum. Three months ago my mum's boyfriend, Tommy, came to live with us. I don't get on with him, he always seems to be finding fault with me and picking on me. Since he moved in he has begun to sell drugs to people who call at the back door. He tries to hide it but I have seen the stuff in my mum's room. I don't like drugs and am afraid that my mum will get into trouble with the police. If I tell my dad what's happening he will go crazy, he'd probably kill Tommy. What can I do? Should I tell my dad or is there anything else I can do? I'm desperate, please help.

Richard

7.2 Dave's Letter

15 Park Drive
Willowbend
Cleveland

Dear John

My mate and I are both 14 years old and go to the same school. There is a group of boys in our year who throw their weight around a lot. They pick on lots of people but especially on us. We get called all sorts of names because we both go to Scouts. I think Scouts is great, next month we are going climbing in the Brecon Beacons in Wales. The thing is, my mate says that he is getting fed up with all the name calling at school and is going to give up Scouts and try and get on the good side of this other group by being more like them. He says 'if you can't beat them you might as well join them'. This crowd seem to spend most of their time just hanging around and causing trouble, I have heard that they all use cannabis and speed and try other things. I don't want my mate getting into that. What shall I do? Please help!

Dave

7.3 Erin's Letter

The Coach House
Mill Cross Lane
Sayerstown

Dear Holly

I am nearly 14 and go out with a really great boyfriend called Cameron. He is 17 and used to go to our school. He used to get in a lot of trouble because the teachers picked on him. He can't get the sort of job he wants and so he stays in bed all morning. He really loves me and treats me like an adult. He says that we should have sex because that would mean that we really love each other. I know he smokes a bit of dope and he lets me have a puff sometimes, although I don't like him using it because he gets moody afterwards. He keeps asking me to lend him money and has even said I could nick money from my dad's shop for him. I really love him but I'm not sure what I should do. What do you think?

Erin

7.4 Jamelia's Letter

30 Bells Crescent
Bournebrook
Testerton

Dear Nathan

Please help me, I am going crazy and am really confused. I am just 14 and have a brother who's 16. He sniffs lighter gas all the time and gets right out of his head. He spends all of his money on cans of gas and sits up in the subway near our house with his mates every evening and sniffs it. He sprays it straight in his mouth. I heard that doing that is dangerous. I tried to tell him but he told me to mind my own business and hit me in the face. He's always in trouble at school and at home. We live with my dad since my mum left and I don't think my dad knows. It would kill him, he tries so hard to be both mum and dad to us. Should I tell him about my brother? What should I do? Is it dangerous like they say?

Jamelia

7.5 Ravi's Letter

The Bell House
Church Close
Tensingbury

Dear Deepak

I really need your help. There is no one else I can turn to and if you can't help I don't know what I'm going to do. I'm 15 and an only child and, the thing is, over the past three months I've got into sniffing aerosols. It started as a dare with some of my mates at a party one night. We all had a go and got out of our heads. I tried it again the next night at home and really liked it. Anyway now I'm getting through several aerosols a day. My parents are out at work during the day and go out most evenings so I have been able to hide it from them. I'm spending a lot of money on it now and have to steal some of it from home to buy enough cans. My parents would kill me if they found out. I think I need help, I feel really rough most of the time and can't stop. I feel so rough some mornings that I don't get to school and I think that my parents will find out soon. What shall I do? Please help.

Ravi

7.6 Denzel's Letter

27 Kings Road
Millsborough

Dear Francis

I am in Year Ten at my school and there is a girl in my year who is
selling drugs at school. She gets them from her older mates and
sells them to other kids at our school. She even sells them to much
younger kids. I don't think she pushes them on anyone but she just
lets it get around that she has them if anyone wants them. I'm not
too sure but she seems to have all sorts of drugs, even hard ones,
for sale. I don't like what she is doing but I don't want anyone to
think that I'm a sneak or a dobber so I couldn't tell a teacher. What
should I do? I'm really worried about it.

Denzel

Exercise 8

What About Us?

Suggested age: 13+ • Suggested lenth of exercise: 45 minutes to 1 hour

Outline

An exercise to encourage participants to consider who in society is affected by others who use drugs, and to examine the degree and seriousness of that effect.

Purpose and expected outcome

- To increase participants' awareness and understanding that drug use, either their own or that of others, not only affects the user, but has wider implications and effects for those around them.

- To encourage participants to consider the effects that drug taking has on society as a whole.

- To encourage individual responsibility over drug decisions.

- To challenge attitudes to drug use.

- To reinforce drug prevention messages.

Method

The teacher or group leader should briefly outline the exercise and split the class into small groups. The blank target worksheet (8.1) should then be distributed and participants instructed to list the names of those individuals or groups who are, in their opinion, affected by someone else's drug use. They should then be told to write the number of the person or group whom they consider is most affected closer to the bull's-eye of the target, and those less affected further away.

After sufficient time has elapsed for this part of the exercise the groups should report back to the rest of the class their list and its order of importance. The teacher can transfer this list to the board or perhaps to a projected image of the bull's-eye. Other members of the class should be encouraged to question the inclusion of particular individuals or groups of persons on any list, and also the positioning. Once all of the groups have reported back it may be possible to draw up a class list where there are areas of agreement. The answer sheet for 8.1 can be used as an example or as a basis for your own ideas. A general discussion can then be held on the way in which those people on it or the lists produced by the class are affected by drug use, and what the possible consequences of those effects might be.

Notes for teacher or group leader

The class can be provided with examples from the suggested list to start them off, if that is considered necessary. They should be encouraged to think of all of the possibilities and not to restrict their thinking just to their immediate circle of family, friends and associates.

Follow-up exercises

Participants could enter into the role of one of those identified as being affected by someone else's drug use, and look closely at the ways in which they personally would be affected and the consequences arising from such effects.

8.1 Those Affected By Drug Use

Make a list, in any order, of those whom you think can be affected by a person's drug use. Write the item number in the position on the target that you think is appropriate, placing those most affected closest to the centre.

1.	8.	15.
2.	9.	16.
3.	10.	17.
4.	11.	18.
5.	12.	19.
6.	13.	20.
7.	14.	

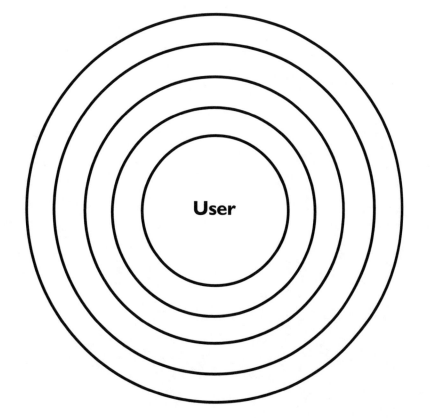

Suggested Answers for Worksheet 8.1

Make a list, in any order, of those whom you think can be affected by a person's drug use. Write the item number in the position on the target that you think is appropriate, placing those most affected closest to the centre.

1. Partner/parents
2. Children
3. Brothers and sisters
4. Family
5. Close friends
6. School/college
7. Neighbours

8. Community
9. Victims of crime
10. Colleagues
11. Employees
12. Employers
13. Taxpayers
14. Health service

15. Street cleaners
16. Insurers
17. Police
18 Courts
19. Social services
20. Prisons

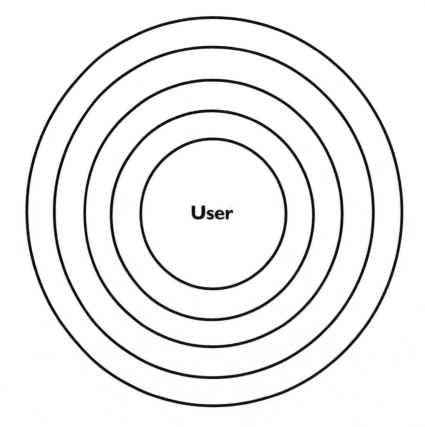

Drug Diamond Nine

Suggested age: 12+ • Suggested length of exercise: 45 minutes to 1 hour

Outline

An exercise to encourage participants to examine pressures, temptations and reasons that lead young people to start or to continue using drugs. It also looks at the corresponding pressures, temptations and reasons preventing many young people from using drugs or that encourage current users to stop.

Purpose and expected outcome

- To enable the examination of issues that affect drug-use decisions.
- To place such issues in order of their importance.
- To encourage participants to consider the drug decisions of others.
- To challenge attitudes to drug use.
- To reinforce drug prevention messages.

Method

The worksheets (9.1 and 9.2) should be copied and cut up to produce sufficient sets for small group work. If it is intended that the sets should be used repeatedly they can be laminated. The teacher or group leader should briefly outline the purpose of the exercise, and split the class up into small groups. The cards that deal with reasons to start or continue drug use (9.1) should be distributed, one set to each group. Groups should be asked to consider the reasons printed on each card and to select nine of them that, in their opinion, represent the most powerful pressures, temptations or reasons for a young person to start drug use or for an existing user to continue. Each set includes a blank card that can be used by the group to include a reason that they feel has been omitted. Having selected nine cards the group should then arrange them in the 'diamond nine' layout, as shown.

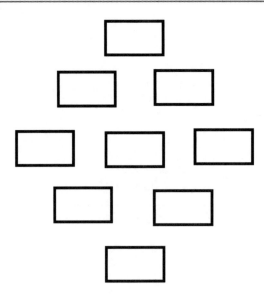

The top position should be occupied by the card that, in the opinion of the group, contains the most important and powerful reason to start or continue drug use. The two positions in the second row should be occupied by the cards that contain the next most important or powerful reasons, the middle row the three next most important and so on, until the bottom position is filled by the card that contains the least important reason.

When sufficient time has elapsed for each group to arrange its cards in a diamond nine, they should report their choice and placings back to the rest of the class. A simple scoring system can be used to arrive at a common diamond nine. The card placed at the top by any group should be awarded one point, cards placed in the second row two points and so on down to the bottom card which should be awarded five points. Cards not selected for inclusion in any group's diamond nine should be awarded six points. When all of the groups have reported back, the points can be added up to produce a common placings list. The card that scores the lowest number of points should be placed at the top, the next two in the second row and so on until the common diamond nine is complete. The cards that have the highest scores are left out. The teacher can then ask each group why they chose to place a particular card where they did. Groups can also be asked to justify leaving out certain cards or placing them in a lower position. General discussion can then take place.

The exercise involving cards containing pressures, temptations and reasons for young people not to start drug use, or for existing users to stop their drug use (9.2), can be used in exactly the same way. The exercise can be performed immediately following the previous diamond nine exercise or on a separate occasion.

Notes for teacher or group leader

There are no totally right or wrong answers in this exercise. It is an opportunity for participants to discuss their views and, having come to an agreement, indicate their reasoning. Providing the group has given sufficient thought to the placings and are prepared to explain their reasoning, then any placing order is valid. When a group is unable to agree a particular placing, then a simple vote may resolve the dispute. When a dispute is not resolved by voting, then a separate minority placing order may be accepted. Every effort, however, should be taken to achieve agreement.

Follow-up exercises

1. Participants could create a set of reasons for becoming involved in other forms of risk-taking behaviour; for example, climbing, canoeing, surfing, theft or vandalism.

2. Participants could be asked to look at how such pressures, temptations and reasons exert their influence over young people.

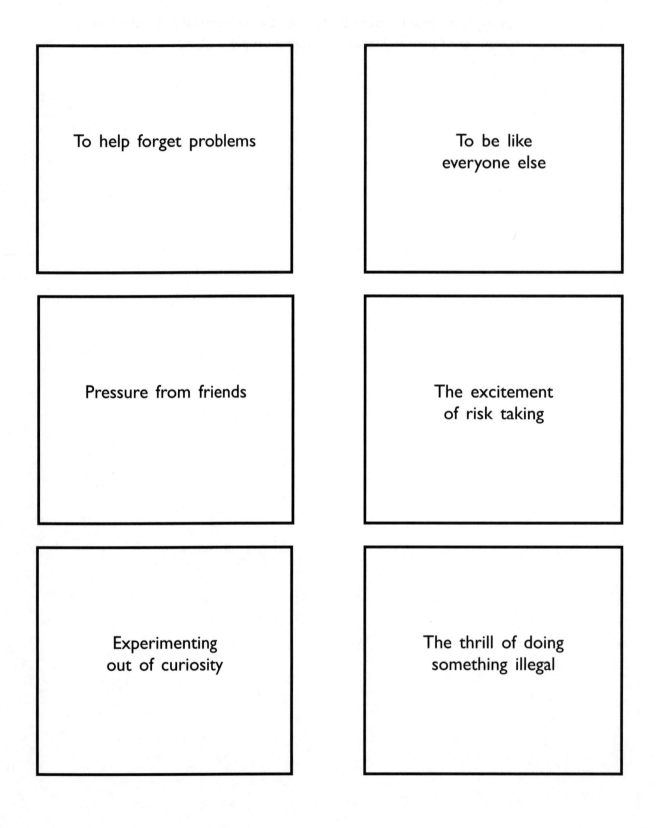

9.1 Reasons to Start or Continue Drug Use (1)

To help forget problems

To be like everyone else

Pressure from friends

The excitement of risk taking

Experimenting out of curiosity

The thrill of doing something illegal

9.1 Reasons to Start or Continue Drug Use (2)

<table>
<tr>
<td>

To join in with
a group

</td>
<td>

You only get a caution if you
get caught

</td>
</tr>
<tr>
<td>

To have a good time

</td>
<td>

Everyone is doing it

</td>
</tr>
<tr>
<td>

Because just trying
them never hurt anyone

</td>
<td>

</td>
</tr>
</table>

9.2 Reasons to Stop or Not to Start Drug Use (1)

Media reports of drug use	The death of a friend
Getting caught by the police	A girl/boyfriend who disapproves
A bad personal drugs experience	Parents finding out

9.2 Reasons to Stop or Not to Start Drug Use (2)

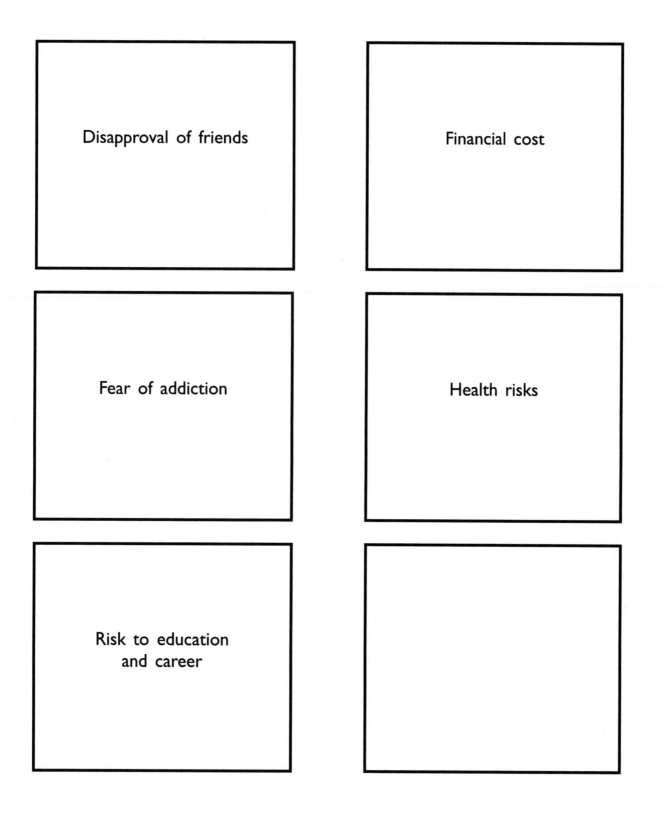

Disapproval of friends

Financial cost

Fear of addiction

Health risks

Risk to education
and career

Exercise 10

Benefits and Drawbacks

Suggested age: 13+ • Suggested length of exercise: 45 minutes to 1 hour

Outline

An exercise to enable participants to consider the benefits and drawbacks of illegal drugs and medicines or prescription drugs and to compare the two.

Purpose and expected outcome

- To encourage the consideration of potential problems associated with illegal drug use.

- To increase the participants' understanding of the possible outcomes of drug use.

- To encourage individual responsibility over drug decisions.

- To challenge attitudes to drug use.

- To reinforce drug prevention messages.

Method

The teacher or group leader should briefly outline the exercise and then split the class into small groups. The groups are issued with the blank worksheets (10.1 and 10.2) and are then asked to consider all of the possible benefits and drawbacks that can be associated with the use of illegal drugs, and with medicines and prescribed drugs. The groups should be encouraged to think deeply about the subject, and to consider as many issues as possible, drawing up lists on the respective worksheets.

After sufficient time has been allowed, each group should report back to the rest of the class the issues on their lists. Groups can be restricted to a small number of issues so that each can make a contribution. The suggested issues can be drawn up as a class list on the board.

When each group has made its contribution, a general discussion of the points raised and their importance can follow. The class should then be asked to rearrange the issues in order of importance.

Notes for teacher or group leader

Two answer sheets for 10.1 and 10.2 are provided that can be used to add extra items into the lists produced by the groups. The exercise can be carried out as an individual activity with each participant being issued with a blank worksheet or, alternatively, the blank worksheets can be produced as overhead transparencies and projected onto a white board. The whole class can then contribute while the teacher enters the suggested items onto the projected worksheets.

Follow-up exercises

1. Participants can be asked to collect newspaper reports of incidents where either illegal or legal drugs have caused problems.

2. Participants can be asked to collect instruction leaflets from various medicines and prescribed drugs, and then to compare the amount of information that is provided by such leaflets with the amount of good factual information that is made available by suppliers of illegal drugs.

10.1 Illegal Drugs

Benefits

Drawbacks

Suggested Answers for Worksheet 10.1

Benefits	Drawbacks
Readily available	No quality control
May give desired effect	Uncertain strength
No prescription needed	High cost
To some they may appear 'cool'	Mixed with other substances
	Not medically tested
	No specified dose
	May lead to criminal charge
	Addiction
	Tolerance
	Withdrawal symptoms
	'Snidey' drugs
	Unpredictable effects, even after previous use
	Supply may be cut off
	No medical supervision
	Danger of overdose
	If injected, can lead to other health problems
	No comeback if dissatisfied

10.2 Medicines and Prescribed Drugs

Benefits

Drawbacks

Suggested Answers for Worksheet 10.2

Benefits	Drawbacks
Known strength	Need to consult a doctor
Medically tested	Can be misused
Known and predictable effects	Some can be addictive
Low cost to user	Prescription costs
No adulterants	
Constant supply	
Supervised use	
Not usually injected	
No 'snideys'	
No legal risks if prescribed for user	
Redress available for poor quality or bad effects	
No involvement in crime	

Exercise 11

Scenarios

Suggested age: 14+ • Suggested length of exercise: 1 hour

Outline

An exercise to encourage participants to look at what other options are available to people who are facing difficulties or pressures in their lives, rather than the use of drugs.

Purpose and expected outcome

- To enable participants to explore possible ways of avoiding dangerous situations.

- To encourage participants to examine the sources of help that are available to those experiencing difficulties.

- To encourage individual responsibility over drug decisions.

- To challenge attitudes to drug use.

- To reinforce drug prevention messages.

Method

The teacher or group leader should briefly outline the exercise and split the class into small groups. Each group should be issued with a copy of one of the scenarios. They should then be asked to discuss the scenario and to answer the following questions:

1. How could the person in the scenario have avoided getting into the particular situation?

2. Where could the person have gone for help or advice?

3. What are the possible further problems that the person might face if the situation does not change?

4. Now that the person is in the situation, what can he or she do to change it?

5. Where might the person go to seek help and advice?

The session leader should allow sufficient time for the group to consider all of the possibilities in the situation, and then ask them to report back to the rest of class the various points that they have discussed, and the solutions that they have come up with. The rest of the class can comment upon the points raised and the suggested solutions.

Notes for teacher or group leader

The session leader will need to be aware that some of the participants may be in personal circumstances that are closely similar to those in the scenarios, and will need to be sensitive to this. It may be advisable to remove a particular scenario if this is felt to be too 'close to home' for any member of the class.

This exercise can be used as an individual exercise with participants being asked to consider and answer one or a number of scenarios, verbally or in writing. As an alternative the leader can read one of the scenarios to the class and then hold a general discussion on the points that it raises, and take suggested answers from the class to the questions posed earlier.

A list of helping agencies that might be able to offer help and advice is given as an appendix to this book.

Follow-up exercises

1. Participants can be asked to research and draw up a list of national or local helping agencies that offer advice in these types of situation.

2. Participants can be asked to collect newspaper reports of real life drug-related situations and to discuss them in the same way as they have discussed the scenarios.

11.1 Teresa

Teresa is a young mother aged 24. Her husband, Richard, works away, sending money home from time to time. Teresa cannot manage on the money she receives, especially as she has three young children who constantly need new clothes, shoes, etc. She feels that she cannot talk to her husband, and gets no support from her family. She is quite shy and hasn't really made friends with anybody in the village where she lives. She has taken to drinking alcohol to ease her anxiety, but this is eating into her inadequate budget. She receives a Valium prescription from her doctor, but uses more than the stated dose. As she feels depressed, she has been considering using street 'speed' like she did when she was 18, as this seemed to lift her mood.

11.2 Kamal

Kamal is 11 and has just started secondary school. He is small for his age and gets picked on by older boys who push him around and steal his belongings. He is too frightened to tell anybody about this – especially his father, who is very strict – and he feels that telling his mother might worry her too much. In order to help him cope with all the pressure, Kamal sniffs lighter fuel from a plastic bag under a bridge by the local canal, usually straight after school.

11.3 Gavin

Gavin is 16 and lives with his parents. Recently his first real girlfriend, Sandra, left him for one of his friends, since when he has become more and more depressed and withdrawn. He has become friendly with another boy who supplies him with speed and LSD, which Gavin uses daily to try and get on with his life. Although he feels OK when he is using the drugs, he feels much worse when the effects wear off. He has begun to shoplift and to steal money from home in order to pay for his new habit. His homework is also suffering and recently he was suspended for a week for swearing at a teacher.

11.4 Tara

Tara is 18 and attends college. She made friends with a crowd who go clubbing at weekends and quickly got into using ecstasy. She now has a tolerance to the drug and is using eight tablets every weekend, which she told her supplier is costing her too much. He suggested that she might start earning some money by supplying the drug to other friends of hers, which she did. Unfortunately, she was caught last week by the police and will have to go to court charged with supplying. Her parents have found out and are threatening to throw her out, and the college have also found out and may expel her.

11.5 Michael

Michael is 35 and gets very agitated and worried about his new job, which he finds too much for him. At the end of the day he can't wait to get home, but once there he just worries about the next day. He is not sleeping very well and has started to smoke cannabis in the evening to help him relax and to sleep. In the morning he is not in a fit state to drive to work, let alone do his job. He has started to make mistakes in his work and colleagues have begun to make comments about it.

11.6 Maya

Maya is 20 and lives alone. Since she lost her job she has started to use heroin and, because of developing tolerance and in order to get the greatest effect from it, has started injecting. She does not like injecting but sees little choice. Her habit is now very expensive and she now works as a prostitute in order to pay for it. Many of her clients offer her extra money to have sex without using a condom and she often agrees.

11.7 Danny

Danny is just 18 and lives with his aunt. His parents split up two years ago. He has a job and goes out with friends most weekends to dances and raves where he uses LSD and ecstasy and sometimes 'speed'. Lately he has been experiencing some strange feelings and thoughts, and believes that he may have done some permanent damage to his brain. This, he feels, is backed up by friends of his who say that he has 'lost it', and that he is 'off his head'. Sometimes he hears voices and feels that he is being watched. He doesn't know what to do. He would like to stop using the drugs but he feels that he can't have a good time without using them.

11.8 Lisa

Lisa recently lost her job at the bank for constantly turning up late with no explanation. She feels that she cannot tell her father, with whom she lives. Her mother left home some years before. She carries on a pretence of going to work by leaving home at the same time every morning. Her father knows that she smokes cannabis, but doesn't really mind as long as she keeps her job. She has now taken to smoking small amounts of heroin during the day, to pass the time and take away her bad feelings. She gets the heroin from an old school friend who is allowing her credit until she can pay him.

11.9 Mandy

Mandy is 21 and currently lives with her boyfriend, Pete, on a traveller's site. They both use speed and heroin, which they inject, and smoke cannabis. Mandy knows that she is three months' pregnant but has not told Pete. She does not know what she wants to do about the pregnancy and is worried about the possible damage that her drug use may be doing to her baby.

11.10 Two 14-Year-Old Boys

Two 14-year-old boys have been taken to hospital from school, as they both became very ill during the lunch break. Nobody seems to know why, but it is believed that they were seen buying some tablets from an older boy who told them that they were a new type of ecstasy.

11.11 Steve

Steve is 14 and lives at home with his parents and two younger brothers. His parents are going through a difficult patch in their marriage and have spoken of divorce. Steve started using lighter gas with some of his friends in the evenings. They all sit in the subway near the shops and have been spraying the gas directly into their mouths. Recently, one of Steve's friends was very ill after using the gas and taken to hospital. The others have all stopped using since then but Steve finds that he can't. He has tried talking to some other friends at school about it but they just told him not to be stupid and to pack it up.

11.12 Martin

Martin is 12 and lives in a children's home. He still sees his mother occasionally but has never seen his father. His mother drinks a lot and can't look after him. He finds it very difficult to make friends with the other children in the home and at school. He spends most of his time on his own and is very lonely and unhappy. Recently, a new boy has moved into the home and seems to like Martin. He spends a lot of time with Martin and makes him laugh. He smokes cannabis and talks of using speed and LSD. He says Martin should use them as well as they would make him feel better. Martin is afraid of what might happen but does not want to upset his new friend.

Exercise 12

In My View

Suggested age: 14+ • Suggested length of exercise: 45 minutes

Outline

An exercise to enable participants to take the role of a person involved in a situation brought about by someone else's drug use, and to consider the options open to such a person.

Purpose and expected outcome

- To encourage consideration of the problems caused to other people involved with and around the drug user.

- To build understanding of how a person's drug use affects others.

- To encourage individual responsibility over drug decisions.

- To challenge attitudes to drug use.

- To reinforce drug prevention messages.

Method

The teacher or group leader should briefly outline the exercise and then split the class into small groups. Copies of the scenarios in Exercise 11 should be distributed, one to each group. Each group should then be issued with one of the worksheets from this exercise. The group is asked to take on the role of the person or group named in the centre of this worksheet and consider the scenario from that viewpoint. They should discuss the situation and then attempt to answer the four questions shown on the worksheet: How would you feel? Whom should you tell? What could you do? What problems will you face? They should be encouraged to look at all possibilities that might flow from their chosen course of action, and then to consider any alternative courses of action. After sufficient time for discussion, each group should be asked to report back to the rest of their class, who should be encouraged to comment on the points raised and the courses of action suggested. The worksheets can then be swapped between groups allowing them to consider the same scenario from the perspective of another person or the scenarios themselves can be swapped. This process can be repeated as many times as the leader wishes.

Notes for teacher or group leader

The teacher leading the session will need to be aware that some of the participants may be in personal circumstances that are similar to those in the scenarios, and will need to be sensitive to them. It may be advisable to remove a particular scenario if this is felt to be too 'close to home' for any member of the class.

The exercise can also be used on an individual basis or carried out with the class as a whole. It could also be set as a written exercise.

A list of helping agencies is provided as an appendix to this book.

Follow-up exercises

Selected scenarios could be acted out, with participants being given the opportunity of taking different roles so that they can explore some of the feelings such persons might experience in situations of this nature.

12.1 Subject of the Scenario

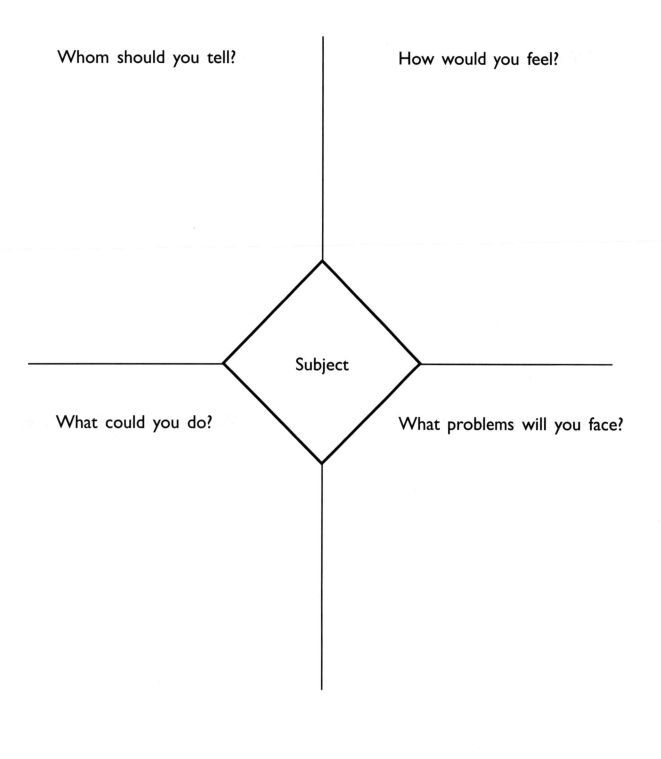

Whom should you tell?

How would you feel?

Subject

What could you do?

What problems will you face?

12.2 Friends of the Subject

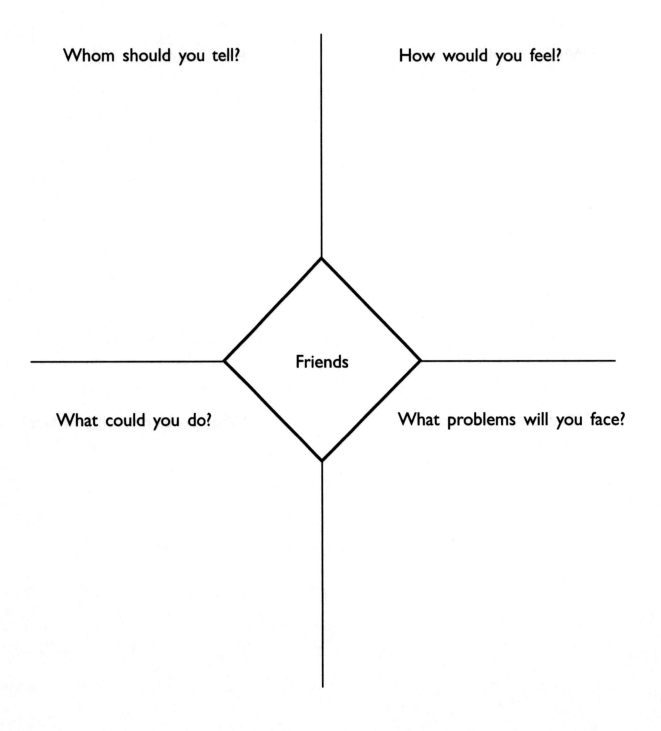

Whom should you tell?

How would you feel?

Friends

What could you do?

What problems will you face?

12.3 Partner of the Subject

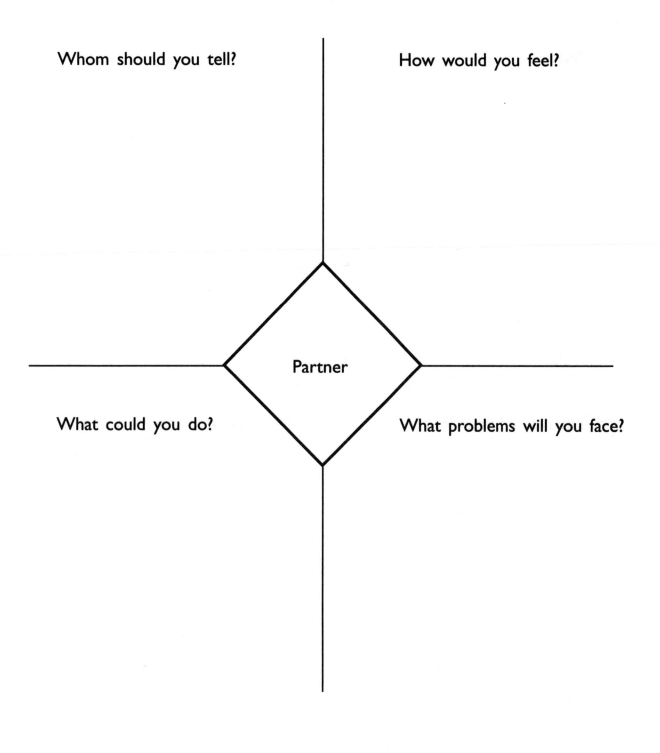

Whom should you tell?

How would you feel?

Partner

What could you do?

What problems will you face?

12.4 Family of the Subject

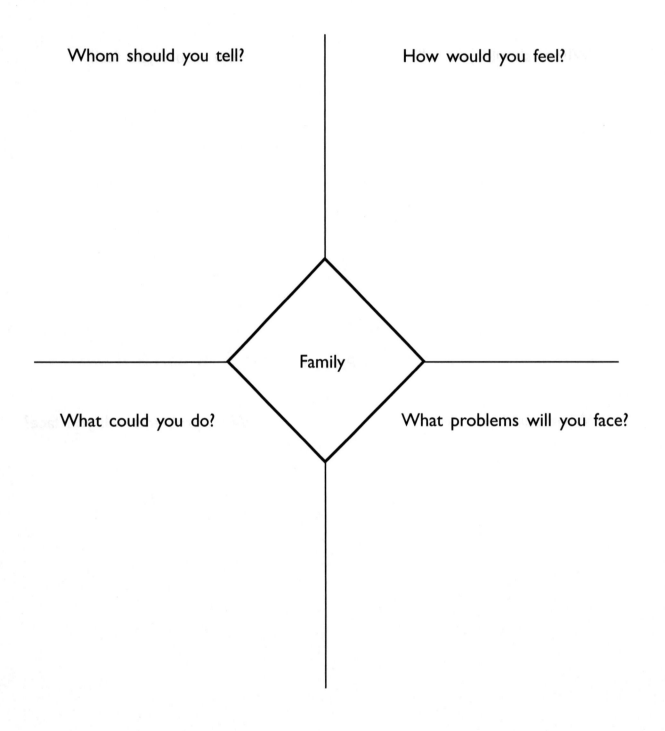

Whom should you tell?

How would you feel?

Family

What could you do?

What problems will you face?

12.5 The Police

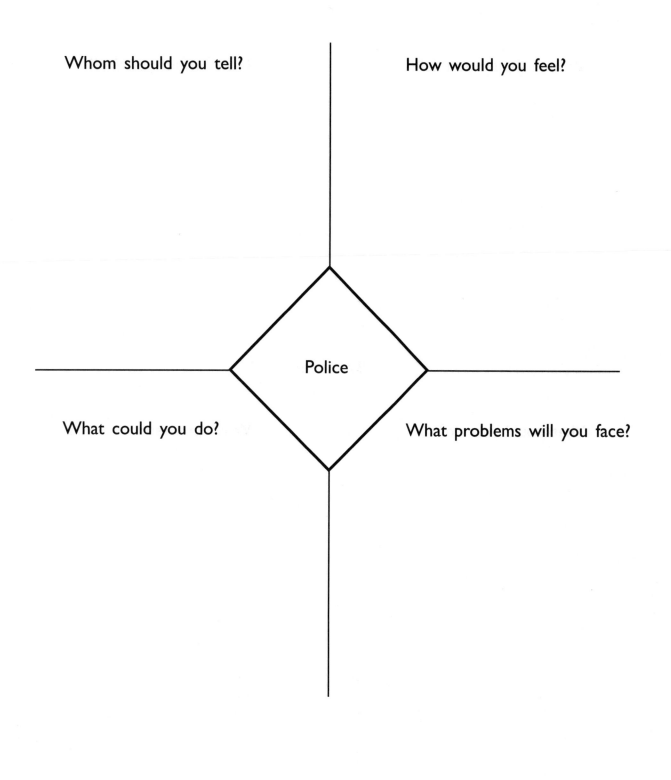

Whom should you tell?

How would you feel?

Police

What could you do?

What problems will you face?

12.6 A Bystander Who Becomes Aware of the Situation

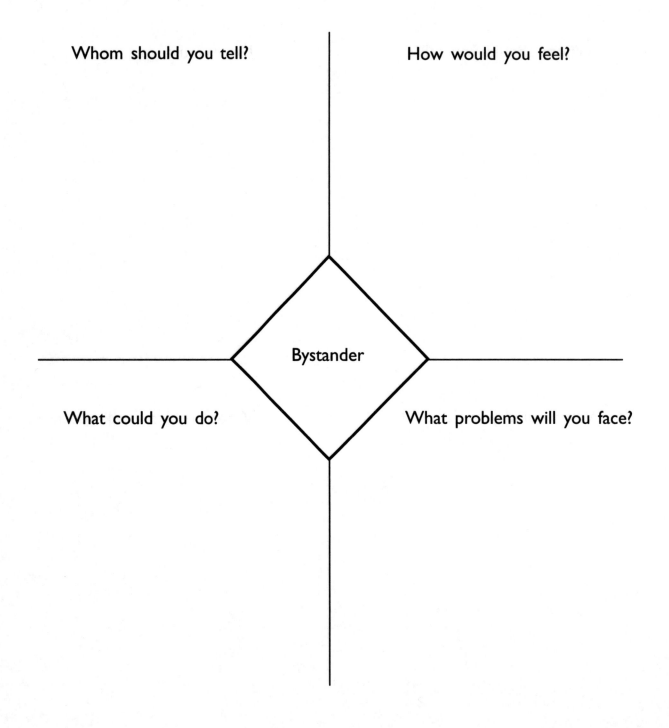

Whom should you tell?

How would you feel?

Bystander

What could you do?

What problems will you face?

Exercise 13

Law and Penalties

Suggested age: 13+ • Suggested length of exercise: 1 hour

Outline

A multi-choice format quiz that enables participants to explore their knowledge of the law as it applies to the use of illegal drugs.

Purpose and expected outcome

- To enable participants to improve their knowledge and understanding of drug laws.

- To clarify some of the myths that surround the law in relation to drug use.

- To prompt discussion of the relevance of the drug laws.

- To encourage individual responsibility over drug decisions.

- To challenge attitudes to drug use.

- To reinforce drug prevention messages.

Method

The quiz sheets (13.1) contain 25 questions designed to be suitable for young people aged 13 years and above. Each question is accompanied by a choice of answers, only one of which is correct.

It should be explained to the participants that the purpose of the quiz is not to examine their level of knowledge about drug laws, but rather to enable them to check out the accuracy or otherwise of the knowledge that they already have, and to add useful and balanced information.

The quiz sheets should be copied and handed out to the participants and time allowed for them to answer the questions. The teacher or leader should then go through the answers using the guidance notes below. Many of the questions will prompt discussion of associated drug issues. This is intended and should be encouraged.

Participants should correct their sheets in line with the given answers and keep them for future reference.

Notes for teacher or group leader

Correct answers

1. Cannabis is a class C drug and possession of it for personal use is punishable on indictment by a term of imprisonment not exceeding **two years**. It is highly unlikely that anyone would receive a sentence of this length for possession of small quantities for personal use. Most adults and juveniles who are found in possession of small amounts of cannabis will receive an official police caution. It has become much less common in recent times for people who have received a drug caution to be given further cautions should they be detected again in possession of drugs. Subsequent appearances at court for cannabis possession can still lead to terms of imprisonment.

2. Generally speaking, a person **cannot** be charged with possession of a drug once it has been taken into the body. It is worth noting that items such as cannabis cigarette butts, bhongs (cannabis water pipes), paper wraps, needles and syringes and scales will normally contain traces of the drug with which they have been used, and will provide enough evidence to base a possession charge on.

3. Passing a cannabis cigarette to a friend for him or her to share most certainly **can** and does lead to charges of supplying the drug. A charge of supplying does not need any money or goods to be exchanged, for the charge is supplying, not selling, and sharing any drug with someone else is considered to be an act of supplying. The maximum penalty for supplying cannabis is 14 years' imprisonment, an unlimited fine and the seizure of all drug-related assets.

4. The active drugs in most varieties of magic or hallucinogenic mushrooms are psilocybin and psilocin. Both of these substances are **class A** drugs. The possession of fresh raw magic mushrooms is not an offence under the drug legislation. It requires some act of preparing the mushrooms for consumption to activate the law. Slicing, crushing, cooking, drying or any other act of preparation would make the offender liable to penalties under class A of the legislation. (See the maximum penalties sheet [17.2] for a complete breakdown of these offences.) It is worth noting that, although the picking of magic mushrooms may not be an offence under the drug laws, it can be considered to be theft under the Theft Act 1968 if permission to pick has not been given by the owner of the land upon which the mushrooms are found. It is also an offence under various pieces of environmental legislation to pick magic mushrooms for sale to others, as most species of magic mushrooms are protected fungi.

5. Using anabolic steroids **is not** a criminal offence. It *is* an offence under the Medicines Act 1968 for an unlicensed person to supply them to someone else.

6. It is **legal** for a person under the age of 16 to buy solvents. The Intoxicating Substance Supply Act 1985 makes it an offence for a person to supply a solvent product to a person apparently under the age of 18 years, if he or she has reason to suspect that the person is going to use the solvents for intoxication.

7. Selling fake ecstasy tablets **is not** an offence under the drug laws. Drug customers are not protected under any consumer legislation. If the seller falsely stated that some tablets were ecstasy, a charge of deception under the Theft Act 1968 might be possible.

8. Possessing needles or syringes **is not** an offence.

9. Parents or any other persons who allow premises over which they have control to be used for the smoking of cannabis **do** commit an offence punishable on indictment by 14 years' imprisonment.

10. You **can** be charged, sent to court and indeed imprisoned on a first drug offence. It is common for people with no previous history of drug offences, found in possession of small amounts of drugs for personal use, to be cautioned by the police, but this is not automatic.

11. It **is** illegal to supply prescription only drugs to others. Some prescription drugs are controlled by the Misuse of Drugs Act 1971 and the rest by the Medicine Act 1968. Both Acts carry heavy penalties.

12. Drivers **can** and often are charged with the specific offence of driving on a road while unfit through the use of drugs. Road traffic accidents caused by drivers affected by drugs are on the increase in the UK.

13. You **could** be charged with GBH if the resultant 'trip' experienced by the unwitting taker of the LSD led to him or her being harmed. You could also be charged with an offence of administering a poison to another person.

14. Supplying heroin, a class A drug, to another person is punishable on indictment by a maximum sentence of **life** imprisonment.

15. The courts **can** confiscate any assets in the possession of drug dealers if they are thought to have been acquired with profits from drug dealing.

16. Drugs **have not** been legalised in the Netherlands. This applies to all drugs including cannabis. The government has decided to 'turn a blind eye' to the cultivation, possession and use of cannabis, but they remain offences under Dutch law.

17. In the UK, doctors **can** prescribe pharmaceutical forms of heroin and amphetamine. While no medical uses of cannabis are currently recognised and doctors cannot prescribe it, this position may change in the future. A number of research programmes is presently under way examining the possible therapeutic use of natural cannabanoids for a number of different medical conditions. Should this research prove fruitful it is likely that natural cannabanoid products would be approved for use in a medicinal form. It is highly unlikely that this would include any smoking form of cannabis. Certain

synthetic cannabanoid drugs are currently approved for medical use and can be prescribed.

18. Poppers (nitrites) **are** legal in the UK with the exception of amyl nitrite, which has recently been outlawed.

19. Dentists **may** use pharmaceutical forms of cocaine as a local anaesthetic, although this practice is now rare.

20. You **can** be sent to prison for a drug offence while pregnant. The fact that a person is pregnant can be taken into consideration when fixing a penalty, but is not a bar to imprisonment.

21. Looking after someone else's drugs **is** an offence. A person doing this is guilty of possession.

22. A person finding an illegal drug **is** allowed to take possession of it to prevent its use. The finder must then dispose of the drug correctly as soon as is practicable. The normal way of disposing is to pass drugs to the police or to a community drug service.

23. If convicted of any drug offence you are very **likely** to be barred from entry or working in many foreign countries. Having a drug conviction can be a very serious impediment in a person's life. The person concerned can find him- or herself barred not only from many foreign countries but also from employment with many companies in the UK.

24. You **can** be charged with offences carried out under the influence of drugs. Acting under such influence is not an excuse and can lead to even heavier penalties being applied.

25. The cultivation of cannabis plants is punishable on indictment by a maximum of **14** years' imprisonment.

Follow-up exercises

The quiz will have raised many issues connected with drug use and the law. Any of these can be followed up with discussions, debates, research projects or essay writing, or in any other way that the group leader sees as being appropriate and useful.

13.1 Law And Penalties (1)

Circle the correct answer.

1. Possession of cannabis for personal use can lead to a sentence of **2 / 5 / 7 / 10 years**.

2. You **can / cannot** be charged with possession of a drug if it is in your bloodstream.

3. Passing a spliff (cannabis cigarette) to a friend for him or her to have a toke, or puff, of **can / cannot** be considered in law to be supplying the drug.

4. The drug in magic mushrooms is a class **A / B / C** drug.

5. Using anabolic steroids **is / is not** a criminal offence.

6. It is **legal / illegal** for a 16-year-old to purchase solvents.

7. Selling fake ecstasy tablets **is / is not** an offence under the drug laws.

8. Possessing needles and syringes for injecting drugs **is / is not** illegal.

9. If your parents allow you to smoke cannabis at home they **do / do not** commit a criminal offence.

10. You **can / cannot** be charged and sent to court for your first drugs offence.

11. It **is / is not** illegal to give prescription drugs to a friend.

12. Drivers **can / cannot** be prosecuted if they drive under the influence of drugs rather than alcohol.

13.1 Law and Penalties (2)

13. You **could / could not** be charged with causing grievous bodily harm for putting LSD in someone's drink without them knowing.

14. Supplying heroin could lead to a prison sentence of **life / 20 / 10 / 5 years**.

15. Money made from the supply or manufacture of drugs **can / cannot** be confiscated by the courts.

16. Drugs **have / have not** been legalised in the Netherlands.

17. In the UK, doctors **can / cannot** prescribe heroin/cannabis/amphetamine.

18. Poppers **are / are not** legal substances.

19. Dentists **may / may not** legally use cocaine on their patients.

20. You **can / cannot** be sent to prison for a drug offence if you are pregnant.

21. Looking after someone else's illegal drugs **is / is not** an offence.

22. A person finding illegal drugs **is / is not** allowed in law to take possession of them.

23. If convicted of a drug offence, you are **likely / unlikely** to be barred from entry into or working in many foreign countries.

24. You **can / cannot** be charged with any offence if it is carried out under the influence of drugs.

25. Growing cannabis plants can lead to a prison sentence of **2 / 5 / 7 / 10 / 12 / 14 years**.

Jigsaw Drugs

Suggested age: 13+ • Suggested length of exercise: 1 hour

Outline

An exercise in which participants reassemble facts regarding particular drugs into an information poster.

Purpose and expected outcome

- To encourage participants to check out their knowledge about certain drugs.

- To give balanced information about drugs and their effects.

- To clarify some of the myths that surround drug use.

- To challenge attitudes to drug use.

- To reinforce drug prevention messages.

Method

The worksheets (14.1–14.12) detail facts regarding a number of drugs or substances of misuse. The leader or teacher should copy the worksheets and then cut them up into their constituent parts. The boxes containing the drug name and its description should be cut out separately. The human figure should be cut into its two halves, one half containing the effects of the drug or substance, the other the problems linked with its use. Finally, the two boxes detailing its method of use and its legal status should be cut out individually. These sections can be laminated if prolonged use is anticipated.

This exercise is intended for use with a small group. The names of the 12 substances should be laid out in front of the group. The 12 descriptions are then dealt to the members of the group as in a card game. Taking turns, each participant is then asked to fit one of their descriptions to its correct substance name. When all of the descriptions have been fitted correctly into place the participants are dealt the left sides of the human figure detailing the effects of the substances. As before, the participants are asked to take turns fitting the sections under the correct name and description. This process is then repeated with the right-hand side of the human figure and the method of administration and legal status sections. The leader should ensure that each section is fitted in its correct place by reference to the worksheet originals. As each section is fitted into place the leader should draw the group's attention to any further points regarding the particular substance under consideration.

The worksheets could also be produced as OHP slides for work with larger groups.

Notes for teacher or group leader

The purpose of this exercise is not to test participants' knowledge regarding individual drugs but rather to allow them to explore and to increase their knowledge and to check out various beliefs and myths.

Detailed information on each of the drugs and substances in this exercise is to be found in the drugs sections of *Understanding Drugs*, the companion volume by the authors of this workbook.

Follow-up exercises

Use the format and information in each worksheet to produce larger posters for classroom display. This could be enhanced by using pictures of real people instead of the human figures. Particular drugs could be researched further, and a complete list of effects and problems created and added to the posters.

14.1 LSD

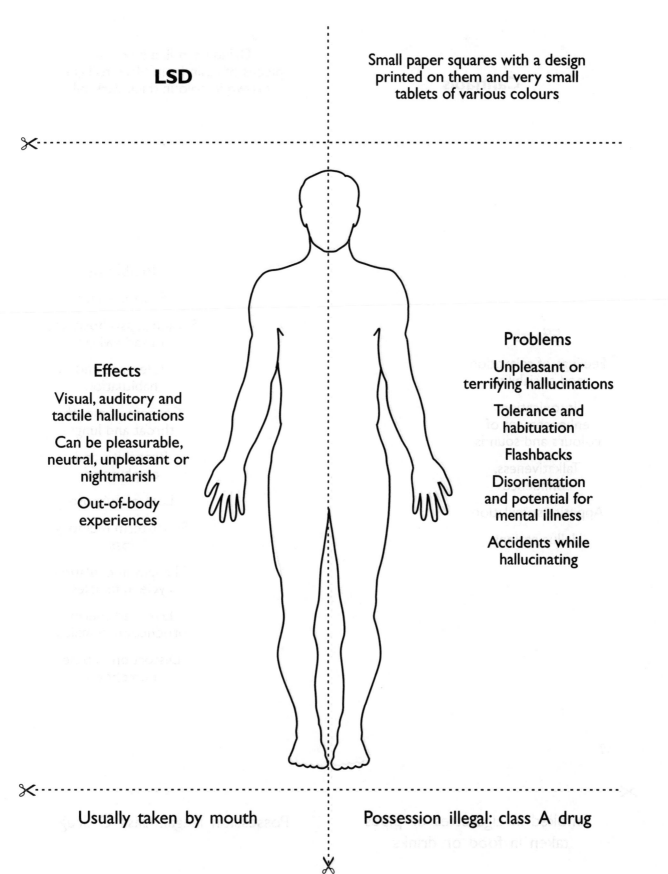

LSD

Small paper squares with a design printed on them and very small tablets of various colours

Effects

Visual, auditory and tactile hallucinations

Can be pleasurable, neutral, unpleasant or nightmarish

Out-of-body experiences

Problems

Unpleasant or terrifying hallucinations

Tolerance and habituation

Flashbacks

Disorientation and potential for mental illness

Accidents while hallucinating

Usually taken by mouth

Possession illegal: class A drug

14.2 Cannabis

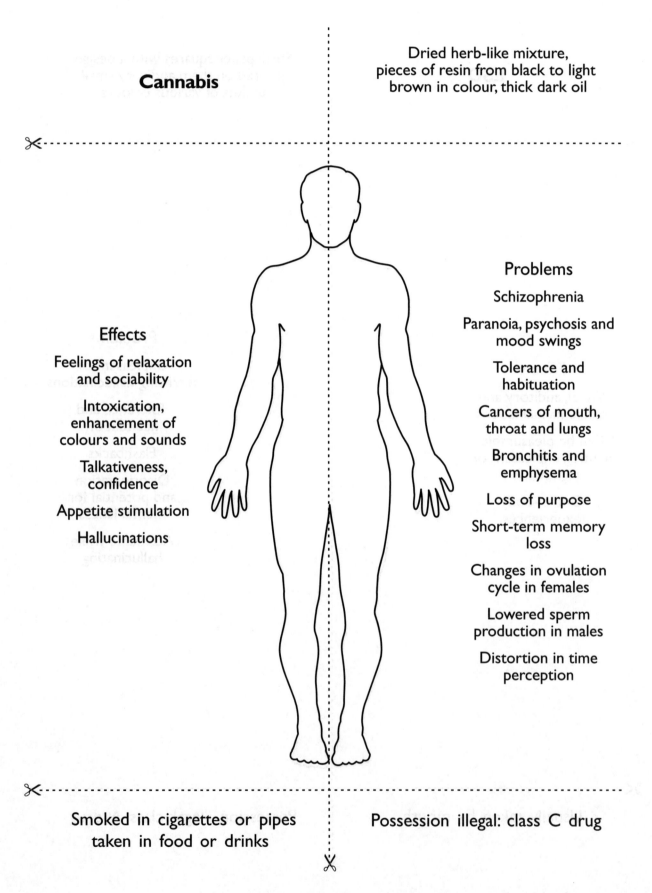

Cannabis

Dried herb-like mixture, pieces of resin from black to light brown in colour, thick dark oil

Effects

Feelings of relaxation and sociability

Intoxication, enhancement of colours and sounds

Talkativeness, confidence

Appetite stimulation

Hallucinations

Problems

Schizophrenia

Paranoia, psychosis and mood swings

Tolerance and habituation

Cancers of mouth, throat and lungs

Bronchitis and emphysema

Loss of purpose

Short-term memory loss

Changes in ovulation cycle in females

Lowered sperm production in males

Distortion in time perception

Smoked in cigarettes or pipes taken in food or drinks

Possession illegal: class C drug

14.3 Amphetamine

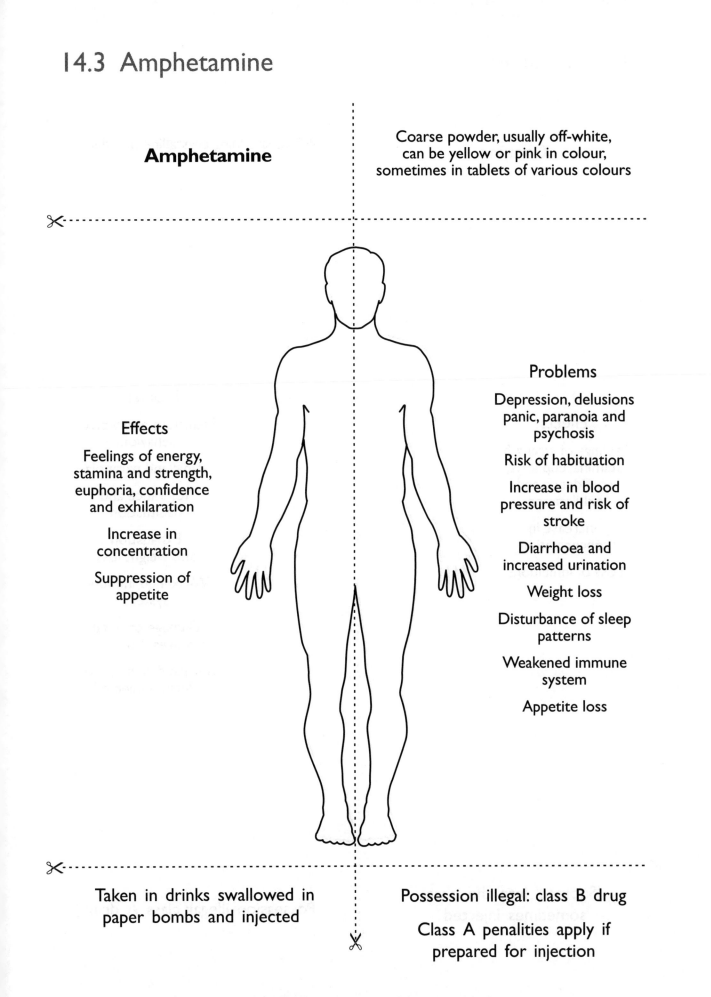

Amphetamine

Coarse powder, usually off-white, can be yellow or pink in colour, sometimes in tablets of various colours

Effects

Feelings of energy, stamina and strength, euphoria, confidence and exhilaration

Increase in concentration

Suppression of appetite

Problems

Depression, delusions panic, paranoia and psychosis

Risk of habituation

Increase in blood pressure and risk of stroke

Diarrhoea and increased urination

Weight loss

Disturbance of sleep patterns

Weakened immune system

Appetite loss

Taken in drinks swallowed in paper bombs and injected

Possession illegal: class B drug

Class A penalities apply if prepared for injection

14.4 Cocaine

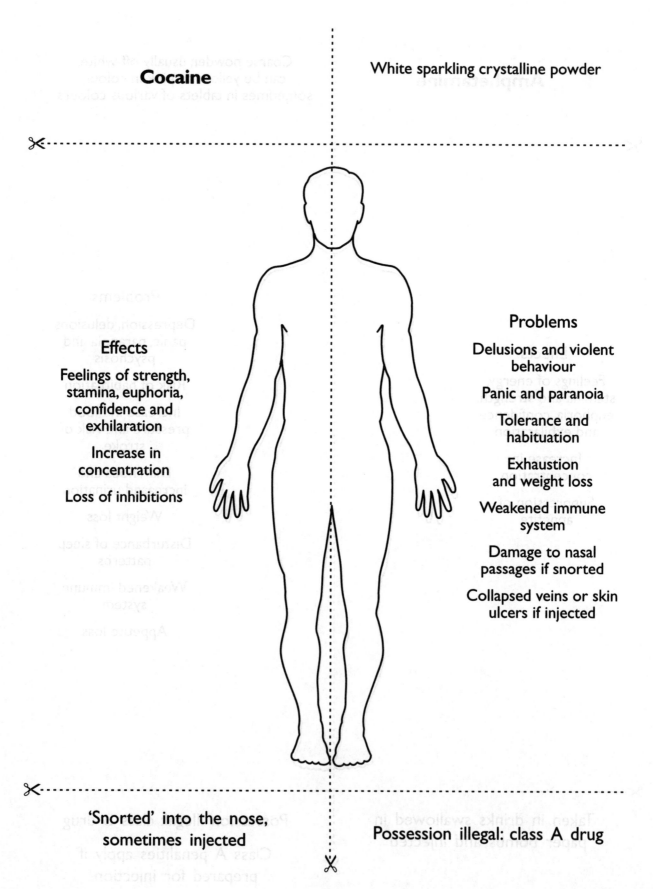

Cocaine

White sparkling crystalline powder

Effects

Feelings of strength, stamina, euphoria, confidence and exhilaration

Increase in concentration

Loss of inhibitions

Problems

Delusions and violent behaviour

Panic and paranoia

Tolerance and habituation

Exhaustion and weight loss

Weakened immune system

Damage to nasal passages if snorted

Collapsed veins or skin ulcers if injected

'Snorted' into the nose, sometimes injected

Possession illegal: class A drug

14.5 Crack Cocaine

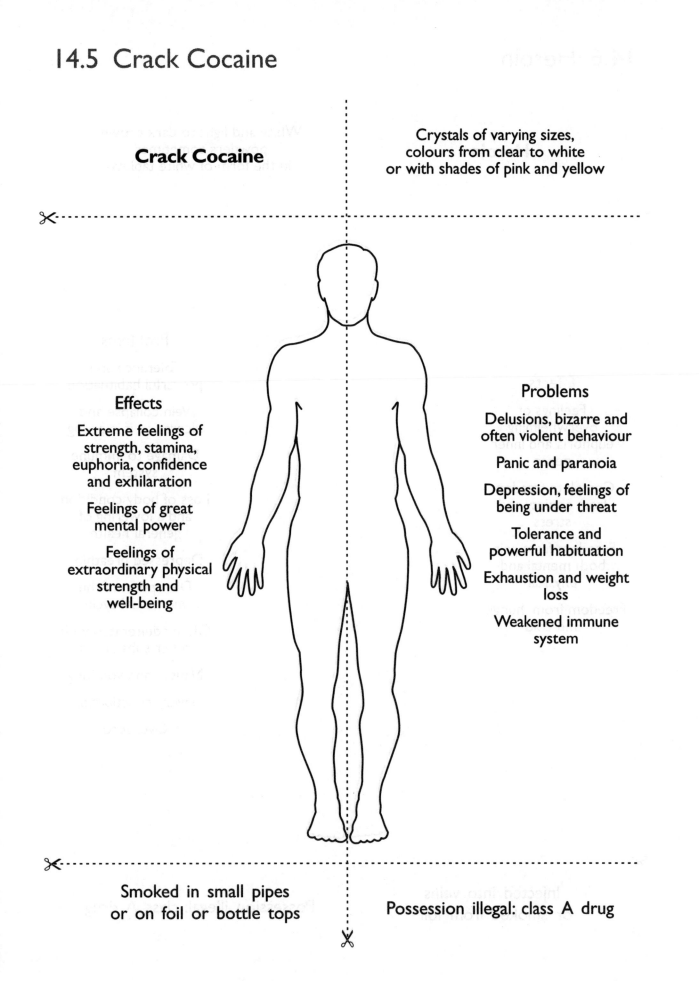

Crack Cocaine

Crystals of varying sizes, colours from clear to white or with shades of pink and yellow

Effects

Extreme feelings of strength, stamina, euphoria, confidence and exhilaration

Feelings of great mental power

Feelings of extraordinary physical strength and well-being

Problems

Delusions, bizarre and often violent behaviour

Panic and paranoia

Depression, feelings of being under threat

Tolerance and powerful habituation

Exhaustion and weight loss

Weakened immune system

Smoked in small pipes or on foil or bottle tops

Possession illegal: class A drug

14.6 Heroin

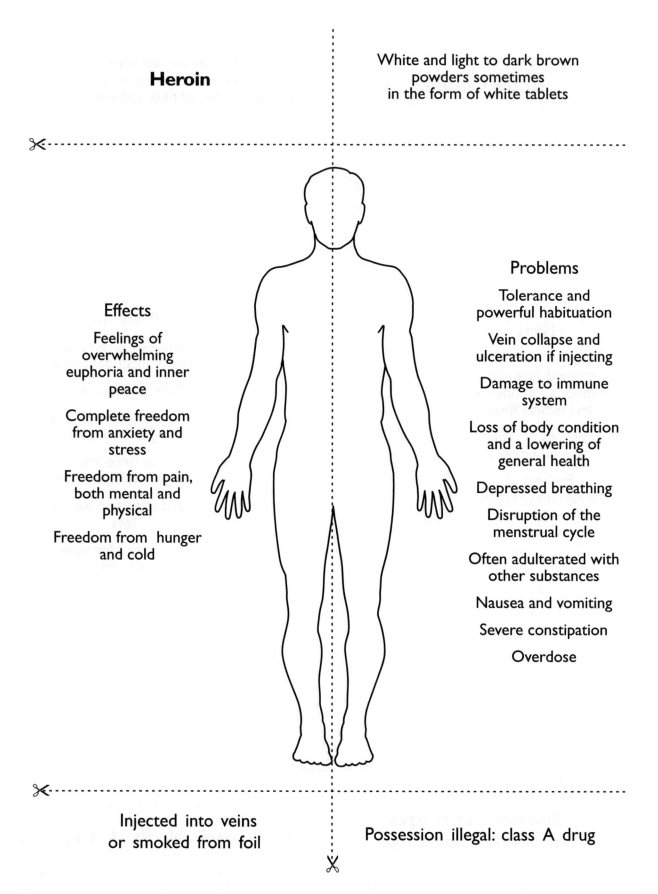

Heroin

White and light to dark brown powders sometimes in the form of white tablets

Effects

Feelings of overwhelming euphoria and inner peace

Complete freedom from anxiety and stress

Freedom from pain, both mental and physical

Freedom from hunger and cold

Problems

Tolerance and powerful habituation

Vein collapse and ulceration if injecting

Damage to immune system

Loss of body condition and a lowering of general health

Depressed breathing

Disruption of the menstrual cycle

Often adulterated with other substances

Nausea and vomiting

Severe constipation

Overdose

Injected into veins or smoked from foil

Possession illegal: class A drug

14.7 Solvents

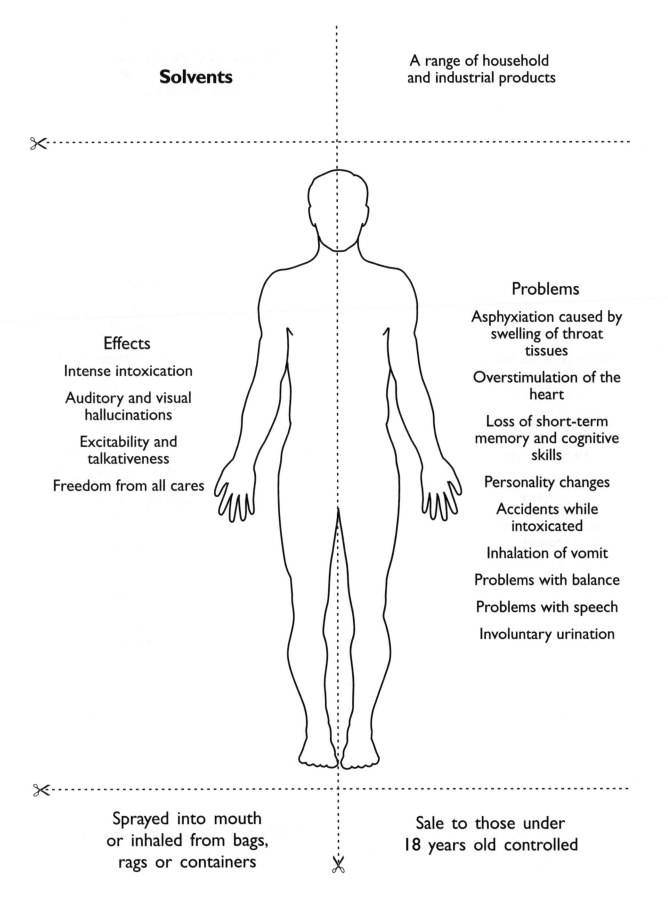

Solvents

A range of household and industrial products

Problems

Asphyxiation caused by swelling of throat tissues

Overstimulation of the heart

Loss of short-term memory and cognitive skills

Personality changes

Accidents while intoxicated

Inhalation of vomit

Problems with balance

Problems with speech

Involuntary urination

Effects

Intense intoxication

Auditory and visual hallucinations

Excitability and talkativeness

Freedom from all cares

Sprayed into mouth or inhaled from bags, rags or containers

Sale to those under 18 years old controlled

14.8 Ecstasy

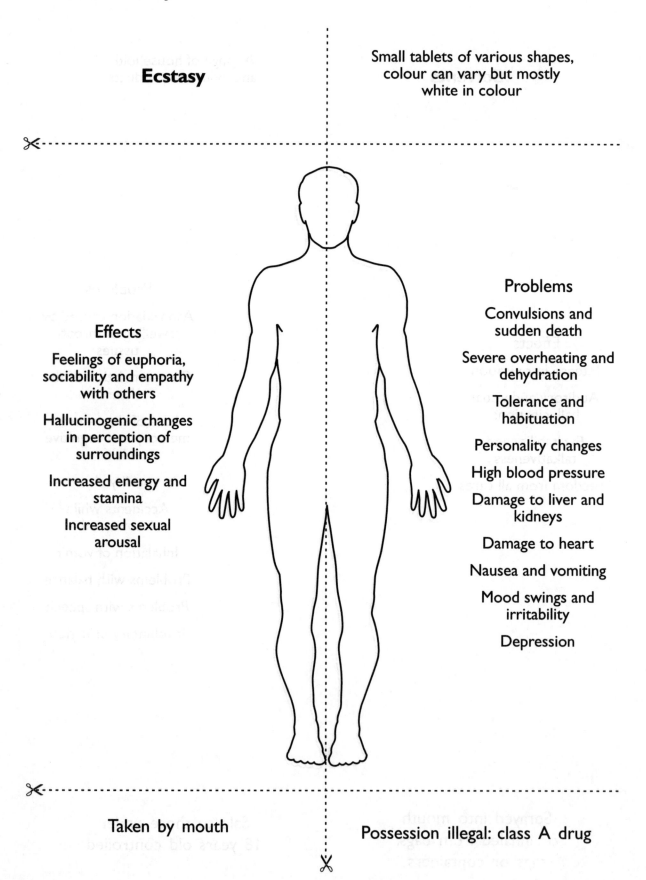

Ecstasy

Small tablets of various shapes, colour can vary but mostly white in colour

Effects

Feelings of euphoria, sociability and empathy with others

Hallucinogenic changes in perception of surroundings

Increased energy and stamina

Increased sexual arousal

Problems

Convulsions and sudden death

Severe overheating and dehydration

Tolerance and habituation

Personality changes

High blood pressure

Damage to liver and kidneys

Damage to heart

Nausea and vomiting

Mood swings and irritability

Depression

Taken by mouth

Possession illegal: class A drug

14.9 Hallucinogenic Mushrooms

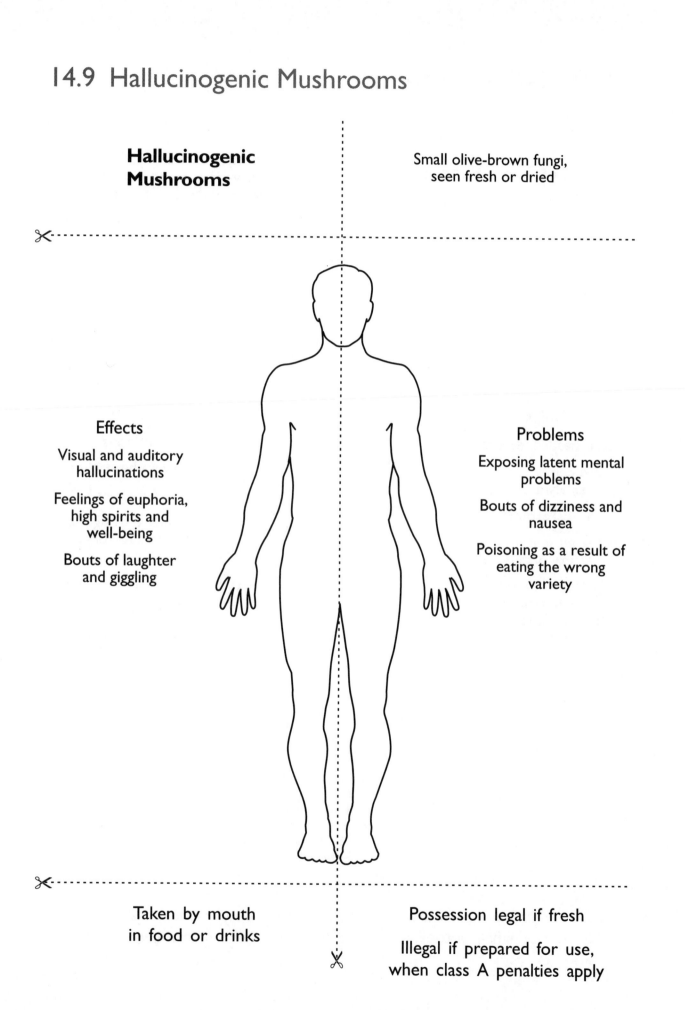

Hallucinogenic Mushrooms

Small olive-brown fungi, seen fresh or dried

Effects

Visual and auditory hallucinations

Feelings of euphoria, high spirits and well-being

Bouts of laughter and giggling

Problems

Exposing latent mental problems

Bouts of dizziness and nausea

Poisoning as a result of eating the wrong variety

Taken by mouth in food or drinks

Possession legal if fresh

Illegal if prepared for use, when class A penalties apply

14.10 Nitrites – Poppers

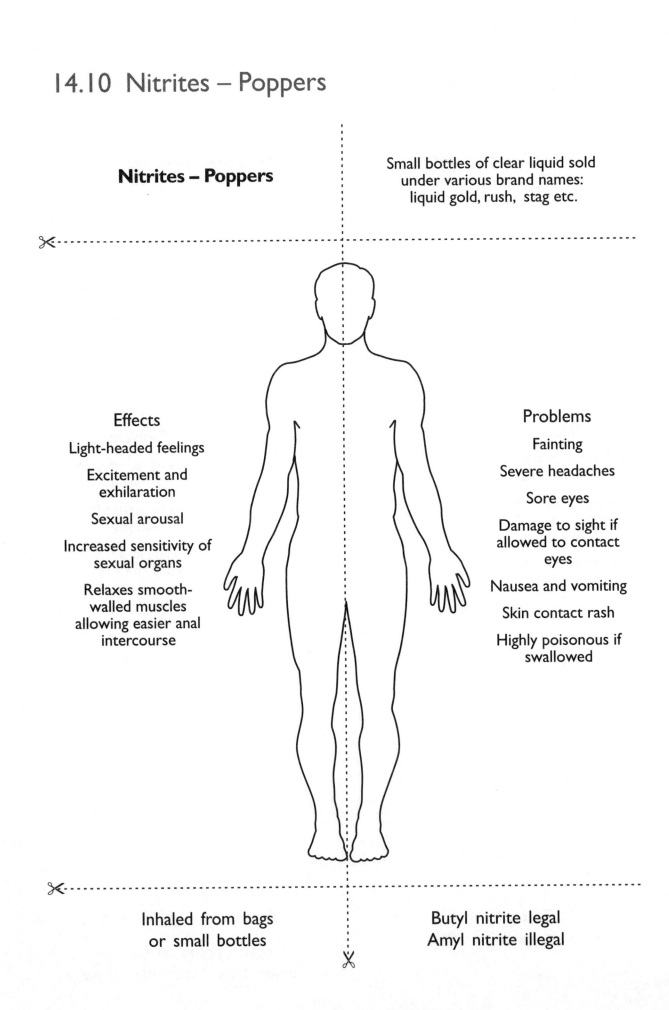

Nitrites – Poppers

Small bottles of clear liquid sold under various brand names: liquid gold, rush, stag etc.

Effects

Light-headed feelings

Excitement and exhilaration

Sexual arousal

Increased sensitivity of sexual organs

Relaxes smooth-walled muscles allowing easier anal intercourse

Problems

Fainting

Severe headaches

Sore eyes

Damage to sight if allowed to contact eyes

Nausea and vomiting

Skin contact rash

Highly poisonous if swallowed

Inhaled from bags or small bottles

Butyl nitrite legal
Amyl nitrite illegal

14.11 Anabolic Steroids

Anabolic Steroids

Ampoules of clear liquid for injection or as tablets and capsules of various colours

Problems

Mood swings, aggression and irritability

Tolerance and habituation

High blood pressure and heart disease

Liver and kidney cancers

Liver and kidney dysfunction

Damage to foetal development

Shrinking of the testicles, impotence

Uncontrollable erections

Bone growth irregularities

Severe acne

Disruption of female's menstrual cycle

Effects

Increase in muscle growth and body bulk when used in conjuction with diet and exercise

Increase in stamina and strength

Injection or by mouth

Use is legal but supply only by prescription, otherwise illegal to supply

14.12 Tranquillisers

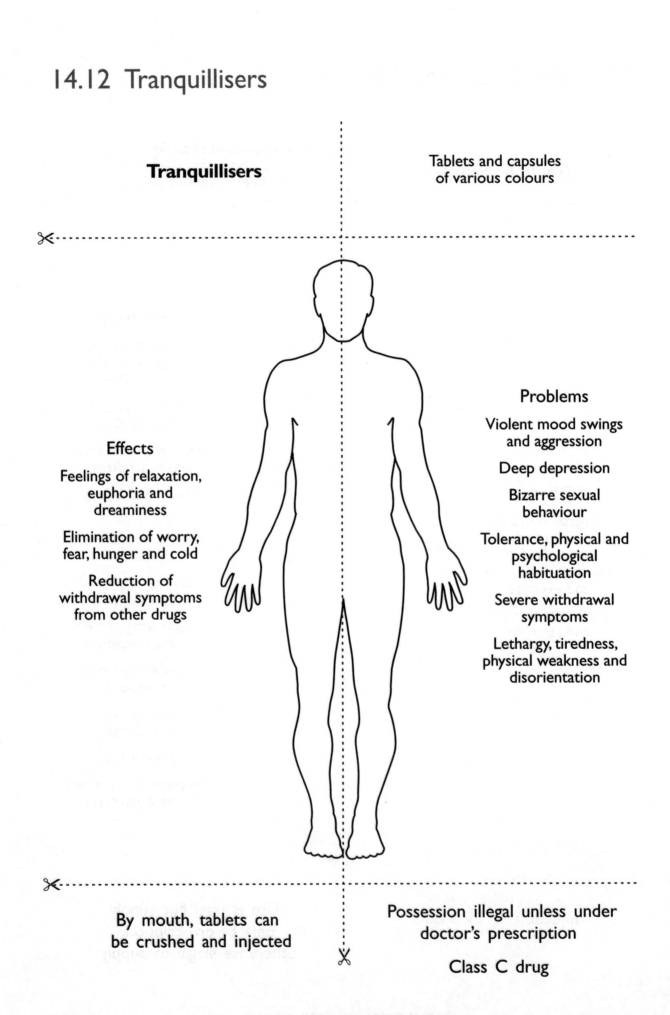

Tranquillisers

Tablets and capsules
of various colours

Effects

Feelings of relaxation,
euphoria and
dreaminess

Elimination of worry,
fear, hunger and cold

Reduction of
withdrawal symptoms
from other drugs

Problems

Violent mood swings
and aggression

Deep depression

Bizarre sexual
behaviour

Tolerance, physical and
psychological
habituation

Severe withdrawal
symptoms

Lethargy, tiredness,
physical weakness and
disorientation

By mouth, tablets can
be crushed and injected

Possession illegal unless under
doctor's prescription

Class C drug

Exercise 15

Health Awareness

Suggested age: 15+ • Suggested length of exercise: 45 minutes to 1 hour

Outline

A multiple format quiz designed to increase participants' awareness of drug-related health issues.

Purpose and expected outcome

- To encourage participants to consider the health implications of drug use.

- To provide accurate information about drugs and health issues.

- To challenge attitudes to drug use.

- To reinforce drug prevention messages.

Method

The quiz comprises 30 questions designed to be suitable for young people aged 15 years and above. Some questions require answers of either 'true' or 'false' while others require more detailed answers. The group leader can decide on the length of the quiz to suit the time available.

It should be explained to the participants that the purpose of the quiz is not to examine their level of knowledge about drugs and health issues but, rather, to enable them to check out the accuracy of the knowledge that they already have, and to add useful and balanced information.

The quiz sheets (15.1) should be copied and handed out to the participants and time allowed for them to answer the questions. The group leader should then go through the answers using the following guidance notes. Many of the questions will prompt discussion of associated issues. This is intended and should be encouraged.

Participants should correct their answers if necessary and keep the sheets for future reference.

Notes for teacher or group leader

Suggested answers

1. **True**. The sharing of injecting equipment can lead to transmission of HIV and Hepatitis B and C, plus other blood-borne diseases. Drug use can increase libido, lower inhibitions and impair judgement, all of which can lead to users becoming involved in unsafe sex.

2. These drugs have been linked to the following mental health problems:

   Amphetamine (speed) – depression, paranoia, anxiety, panic attacks psychosis and schizophrenia.

   Cannabis – depression, anxiety, paranoia, schizophrenia, psychosis.

   Ecstasy – depression, anxiety, paranoia, panic attacks, personality disorders.

   LSD (acid) – anxiety, agitation, panic attacks, personality disorders.

   Cocaine/crack – panic attacks, depression, paranoia, agitation, aggressive personality disorders.

3. These drugs have been linked to the following physical health problems:

   Amphetamine (speed) – suppressed appetite/weight loss, insomnia, impaired immune system, increased blood pressure, low birth weight and malnourishment in infants.

   Cannabis – breathing disorders, cancers, lowered sperm count/impotence, low birth weight in infants, higher mortality in infants.

   Ecstasy – overheating, dehydration, impaired kidney and liver function, damage to brain cells, facial muscle spasm, convulsions.

   Cocaine/crack – damage to nasal tissues if snorted, increased blood pressure, exhaustion, nausea, respiratory problems if smoked, infants born withdrawing from drug.

   Heroin – indifference to pain, suppressed appetite, impotence, constipation, physical addiction and withdrawal, various extra dangers if injected (see below).

   Magic mushrooms – risk of poisoning, vomiting, diarrhoea.

   N.B. If any drug is used intravenously this brings additional problems and risks, such as vein collapse, abscess, blood poisoning, gangrene, infections, etc.

4. **True**. Nitrates were used in the past to relieve the symptoms of angina and to revive people who had fainted (in the form of liquid smelling salts).

5. The higher blood pressure in an artery may prevent injection and can lead to excessive blood loss. Drugs are commonly injected into veins rather than into muscle or arteries because the vein carries blood directly back to the heart for distribution throughout the body. Injecting a drug also produces a much quicker and more intense response than when taken orally.

6. **True**. Research suggests that the high tar content of cannabis, high burning temperature and greater number of recognised cancerous agents in its smoke pose a greater risk of cancer than tobacco use alone.

7. **True**. The most commonly used mushroom, the Liberty Cap, is easily confused with many other varieties, some of which are poisonous. If dried correct identification is almost impossible.

8. LSD is the most powerful psychoactive drug known. Experiences may be negative or positive, and the adverse side-effects can include hallucinations, flashbacks, panic, paranoia, reality distortion, increased accident risk while hallucinating and possible long-term mental illness.

9. **All answers are correct**, depending on degree and length of use, and the testing process used. For example, regular use may be detected in the urine for up to 30 days, whereas testing of human hair may indicate cannabis use for a much longer period.

10. Amphetamine (speed) suppresses appetite and increases metabolism. This can lead to malnutrition of the mother and her foetus, resulting in low birth weight and the risk of physical or mental damage to the unborn child.

11. All legal and illegal drugs that enter the mother's bloodstream, whether smoked, injected, snorted or taken orally, have the potential to cross the placental barrier and adversely affect the foetus.

12. Anabolic steroid use by males can lead to:

    - reduced testicle size (irreversible)
    - aggression ('roid rage'), possibly of a sexual nature
    - acne
    - irregular bone growth (especially in adolescents)
    - liver and kidney cancer
    - raised blood pressure
    - water retention
    - lowered sperm output
    - overdevelopment of breasts (can be irreversible).

13. Anabolic steroid use by females can lead to:

    - enlargement of the clitoris
    - deepening voice
    - growth of facial and body hair
    - male pattern baldness
    - decrease in breast size
    - disruption of menstrual cycle
    - damage to foetus if pregnant.

14. **Physical addiction** – the need to repeatedly use a drug in order to avoid physical withdrawal symptoms, such as stomach cramps, aching joints, flu-like symptoms, insomnia and tremors.

    Psychological addiction – the psychological need to repeatedly use a drug due to feelings of being unable to cope without it. These feelings are usually unfounded but can be powerful.

15. Tolerance is the need to use ever-increasing amounts of a drug in order to obtain the desired effects. Tolerance will build with regular use of a drug, but will quickly fade once use has ceased.

16. **Twenty minutes**. The short duration of effects can lead to repeated use of cocaine.

17. **All are correct**. The duration of the hallucinatory trip can vary widely, and depends on factors such as tolerance, mood of user, environment expectations of user, etc.

18. Street drugs that are found in powder or tablet form are generally adulterated with substances to increase their weight and bulk and, therefore, the supplier's profit margins. Many of these extra substances are of a harmless nature, while others can place the user at some risk, especially if the drug is being injected. Examples of dangerous impurities include brick dust or chalk, which can clog small blood vessels; poisonous substances such as strychnine; or other drugs, which may cause an adverse effect to that expected.

19. **Brain**. Tissue damage and impairment of neurotransmitter action. Overheating caused by the drug can lead to cerebral convulsions and death.

    Kidney. Impairs function of this organ which can result in water retention. Also linked to kidney cancer.

    Jaws. Can cause spasm of facial muscles, leading to a form of lockjaw.

    Heart. Increases heart rate and therefore blood pressure, which can be dangerous for those with cardiac weakness.

    Lungs. Is linked with pulmonary embolisms (blood clots), which can lead to death.

20. Dehydration can result from overheating caused by ecstasy use, which induces heavy perspiration. Dehydration can lead to severe cramps, excess levels of salts in the blood, over-concentration of urine, fainting and collapse. Users of the drug must therefore replace this lost fluid. The current advice is to sip a pint of water each hour, preferably in the form of an isotonic drink.

21. **The adrenal gland**. This results in the overproduction of the hormone adrenaline, which can lead to increased and irregular heart rate and panic attacks. In extreme cases this can result in cardiac arrest and death.

22. The combined effects of two similar types of drug, such as ecstasy and amphetamine (stimulants) or heroin and alcohol (depressants), can lead to life-threatening situations. Two depressant drugs used together can slow the

body's functions to standstill and death. On the other hand, two stimulant drugs used together can lead to overstimulation, overheating, strain on the heart and brain and, again, eventual death. The mixing of dissimilar drugs can lead to unpredictable and potentially dangerous effects.

23. Withdrawal symptoms from heroin include:

- diarrhoea, leading to dehydration and cramps
- aching joints and runny nose
- insomnia
- fluctuations in skin temperature
- headaches
- tremors
- sweating
- muscle spasms.

24. Check **ABC**:

- **airway** – check that airway is open and unobstructed
- **breathing** – check that friend is breathing
- **circulation** – check for pulse or heartbeat.

Move the friend to a **safe environment** if possible and necessary.

Place in **recovery position**.

Check temperature; if the person is hot then attempt to cool, if cold then cover to keep warm.

Reassure by talking, even if you think the friend is unconscious.

Summon help by **999** to ambulance service.

Stay with the friend until arrival of medical help.

Keep any evidence of the substance used and hand it to medical staff.

25. **True**. Literally, 'what goes up must come down'. Stimulant use produces feelings of being 'high' which is always followed by a corresponding 'low', leading in many cases to depression.

26. **Depression** – true.

Withdrawal – true.

Obesity – false.

Acne – false.

Insomnia – true.

Aggression – **true**.

Irregular heartbeat – true.

Sterility – false.

Diarrhoea – false.

27. **Hyperthermia (Overheating)** – ecstasy, amphetamine.

    Weight loss – amphetamine, cocaine.

    Cancer – cannabis, ecstasy, anabolic steroids.

    Paranoia – cannabis, amphetamine, LSD, ecstasy, cocaine.

    Asphyxia – solvents.

    Overdose – heroin, cocaine.

28. The use of certain drugs can lead to an increased libido, a reduction in inhibitions and a loss of judgement and control. This may then place the users in situations where unsafe sex may follow.

29. Both cannabis and steroid use can affect male fertility by reducing the levels of certain hormones and therefore sperm production and motility. The menstrual cycle in women can be adversely affected by the use of ecstasy, steroids or heroin.

30. (a) **True**. Can be used to ward off the withdrawal effects of some illegal drugs; may be misused in their own right for their effects or overused by those who have been prescribed them. Overuse can be as a result of tolerance or the need for an emotional or chemical prop.

    (b) **True**. Many pharmaceutical substances, especially those in tablet, capsule or powder form, can be sold under the guise of other street substances, such as ecstasy, amphetamine, heroin and cocaine.

    (c) **True**. Many pharmaceutical drugs are prescribed for short-term use only. Extended periods of use can lead to both physical and psychological addiction. Abrupt withdrawal from some of these substances can be very dangerous.

Follow-up exercises

The quiz will have raised many health issues connected with drug use. Any of these can be followed up with discussions, research projects or essay writing, or in any other way that the group leader sees as being appropriate and useful.

15.1 Health Awareness (1)

Circle the correct answer or write your answer in the space provided.

1. Drug use can lead to HIV infection.
   True / False

2. Which illegal drugs can lead to mental health problems?

3. Which illegal drugs can lead to physical health problems?

4. Poppers (nitrites) have been used for medical purposes.
   True / False

5. Drugs are commonly injected into veins. Why is this?

6. Cannabis smoking carries a high cancer risk.
   True / False

7. Magic mushrooms can be easily confused with other, more poisonous, varieties
   True / False

8. What are the possible side-effects of LSD use?

9. Cannabis can be detected in the human body for:
   two days / one week / one month / six months two years

10. If pregnant women use amphetamine (speed), how can this affect their unborn chid?

11. Which other drugs can affect unborn infants if their mothers use them?

15.1 Health Awareness (2)

12. What side-effects can occur in men who use anabolic steroids?

13. What side-effects can occur in women who use anabolic steroids?

14. Explain the difference between physical and psychological addiction.

15. Repeated ecstasy use can lead to tolerance. What does this mean?

16. The desired effects of cocaine usually last for:
20 minutes / 2 hours / 6 hours / 12 hours

17. An LSD trip, whether good or bad, can last for:
3 hours / 15 minutes / 10 hours / 24 hours / 45 minutes.

18. How can the impurities commonly found in street drugs affect the user's health?

19. Ecstasy use can have a bad effect on which of the following parts of the body?
brain / kidney / jaws / heart / lungs

20. Why is dehydration a problem for ecstasy users?

21. Which gland is stimulated by solvent use, and how does this affect the body?

22. Why can mixing drugs be especially dangerous?

23. List the physical withdrawal symptoms from heroin.

24. If a friend collapses after using drugs, what steps can you take to help?

25. The use of a stimulant drug such as speed and cocaine can leave you feeling depressed.
    True / False

26. The caffeine content of some soft drinks can lead to which of the following health problems?
    depression / withdrawal / obesity / acne / insomnia / aggression / irregular heartbeat / sterility / diarrhoea

27. The following health problems are associated with which drug or drugs?
    overheating / weight loss / cancer/ paranoia/ asphyxia / overdose

28. What are the links between drug use and unsafe sexual practices?

29. Which drugs affect fertility in males and menstruation in females?

30. Some prescribed drugs can be:
    (a) misused   **True / False**
    (b) sold as other drugs   **True / False**
    (c) addictive   **True / False**

Exercise 16

Just Another Ordinary Day

Suggested age: 13+ • Suggested length of exercise: 1 hour

Outline

An exercise that uses a short but eventful story to promote discussion of a number of potentially dangerous drug-related incidents.

Purpose and expected outcome

- To increase the participants' sense of community responsibility.

- To encourage individual responsibility over drug decisions.

- To see personal drug use in a wider context.

- To challenge attitudes to drug use.

- To reinforce drug prevention messages.

Method

The group leader should outline the exercise to the class and then split them up into small groups. Copies of the story are then distributed to each group and they should be asked to read it and consider the various situations that Mary encounters. The groups should list each incident and the hazards that are apparent. They should also consider what actions Mary might have taken in each case and what her alternative decisions are at each point.

After sufficient time has been allowed, the groups should be asked to report back to the class as a whole the results of their considerations. The rest of the class should be encouraged to comment upon the points being raised.

It may be necessary for the leader to restrict each group's report to a particular incident or a small number of incidents in order that each group has the opportunity to make their report.

When each of the groups has made their reports, the leader should briefly draw together the points made by the class and the lessons that have come out of the exercise.

As an alternative, the story can be read by the leader to the class as a whole, and points raised by individual class members and then discussed.

Notes for teacher or group leader

Mary's life is deliberately brimming with drug-related incidents. It is not intended to represent any sort of typical day, but offers differing sorts of incidents that people may have to face in real life.

Below is a list of questions that the leader might suggest to prompt discussion:

1. Why was Rebecca awake all night? Should Mary seek medical advise?

2. Was it wise to take a double dose of paracetemol? This drug has great potential to cause irreverdible liver damage if used to excess.

3. What are the safety implications of leaving the paracetemol where Rebecca could reach it?

4. What are the possible health immplications of Rebecca handling used needles and syringes?

5. Did Mary dispose of the needles and syringes properly? Needle stick injuries to waste disposal workers are a constant problem.

6. Was Mary right to decide not to tell Ronnie's mother about what she had seen?

7. Were Mary and Dennis right to ignore the girl sleeping in the bus shelter? She might have been in a state of collapse due to alcohol, with the possibility of choking on her own vomit or simply falling from the bus shelter seat.

8. Was Mary right to take the drug that Dennis offered? Would it 'cure' her depression?

9. Is she right to trust Dennis's reassurances over the drug's safety?

10. Was Mary's mother right to suggest giving Rebecca half an adult sleeping tablet?

11. Was Mary right to trust her mother as a babysitter for Rebecca?

12. Was it a good idea to drink a 'couple of vodkas' to cool off? Alcohol has a dehydration effect which may exacerbate any water loss due to overheating.

13. Was she right to take the tablets to avoid feeling 'left out'?

14. What are the implications of Mary's friends not telling the ambulance crew about the drugs she had taken?

15. Was what happened Mary's fault? Where does the responsibility lie?

Follow-up exercises

The story would make an excellent basis for some imaginative role-play work or could be used as a stimulus for written work; for example, a newspaper report on local drug use.

16.1 Just Another Ordinary Day (1)

Mary Brown was having a bad day. The washing machine had broken and her baby, Rebecca, had been awake throughout the night. Mary reached for the paracetamol and initially took two tablets, but then took a further two as she had a splitting headache. She then placed the open bottle on the coffee table near to where Rebecca was playing.

About half an hour later, Mary decided to venture out to the shops with Rebecca, taking the short cut across the park. Rebecca ran on ahead and started to play with some items she found in a flower bed. Mary was horrified to find that Rebecca had found some discarded needles and syringes, and immediately took them and placed them into a wastepaper bin nearby.

Over by the bandstand a boy was acting in a drunken manner. He dropped what looked like an aerosol can and staggered off in the direction of the bridge by the canal that ran alongside the park. Mary knew the boy – he was Ronnie, a neighbour's son – but she decided not to tell the boy's mother as she did not want to get him into any trouble.

On reaching the shops Mary met her friend Dennis, and they talked a while as they watched a group of young people who were drinking in a nearby bus shelter. As they watched, two of the group rode off at speed on a motorcycle towards the motorway and the rest of the group then walked off, leaving behind a girl who appeared to be asleep on her back in the bus shelter. Mary and Dennis shrugged their shoulders at what they saw, but decided that's how young people are today and that it was nothing to do with them.

Mary told Dennis about how awful she felt and how tired she was. Dennis offered to get her something he bought from a friend of his which he said would give her energy and lift her depression. Mary was grateful for this offer, and handed over the money to pay for it. She asked Dennis if he was sure that it would be good for her. Dennis took the money and reassured her.

Once Mary had all of her shopping, she decided to catch a bus over to her mother's house on the other side of town. There they ate a meal, and Mary tried to settle Rebecca down for a nap, but the child was irritable and restless. Mary's mother suggested that they give her half of one of the sleeping pills prescribed by her doctor, but Rebecca would not swallow it.

16.1 Just Another Ordinary Day (2)

Later that evening, Mary asked if her mother would babysit, as she wanted to go out clubbing with some of her friends. The club she went to was the Seventh Heaven at the end of the high street. It became increasingly hot inside as the dance floor began to fill up, and Mary had a couple of vodka and tonics to cool off. Later on, one of her friends came back with some tablets he had just bought and suggested that they all take one to have a good time. Mary was a little unsure, but took one anyway as she didn't want to be left out. She carried on dancing but began to feel hot and dizzy. She went to the toilet and quickly collapsed in one of the cubicles. When she had not returned after 20 minutes, one of her friends went to look for her, and found her lying unconscious.

An ambulance was called and soon after Mary was taken to hospital. None of her friends mentioned what she had taken to the ambulance crew as they did not want to get her into any trouble.

After a few days, Mary was beginning to recover and she was visited by one of her neighbours, who asked her how all this had happened. Mary replied that she couldn't remember, but in any case she was sure it wasn't her fault.

Six Things to Consider

Suggested age: 14+ • Suggested length of exercise: 45 minutes to 1 hour

Outline

A didactic exercise aimed at young people who may have tried drugs, been offered them, or who may soon be placed in a situation where they have to make a decision about them.

Purpose and expected outcome

- To improve the level of young people's knowledge about drugs.

- To encourage responsibility for personal decisions about drugs and their use.

- To reduce the harm caused by certain forms of drug taking.

- To challenge attitudes to drug use.

- To reinforce drug prevention messages.

Method

Worksheet 17.1 shows the six major issues that those who are using drugs may have to face up to. This sheet can be used as an OHP or copied and distributed to the class members as an *aide memoire*, or for them to add notes to, during the lesson. The accompanying notes for the teacher or group leader explain how some of these issues are linked, outlining the dangers and problems associated with each.

The teacher or group leader should outline the purpose of the exercise to the class, and then work through the accompanying notes with them. The class can be encouraged to discuss and comment upon each section of the notes as it is worked through. The discussion on 'illegality' can involve the use of the maximum penalties sheet (17.2).

At the end of the exercise the leader should draw together the main points that have come out of the discussions.

Notes for teacher or group leader

Tolerance

Tolerance to any drug will build rapidly if the drug is used on a regular basis. In order to get the same effect as that achieved initially, greater quantities of the drug must be used on each subsequent occasion. This is because the body becomes accustomed to the drug's use and effects, and tries to even these out by changing its reaction to them. Tolerance will build with the use of illegal street drugs; legal drugs such as alcohol, nicotine and coffee; and even some medical drugs, if used for a long enough period. Tolerance will fade once use of the drug has ceased.

Cost

Once tolerance to a specific drug begins to build, it will necessitate the user buying or obtaining ever-greater amounts of the drug to get the desired effect. This is great news to the dealer or supplier, as he or she will become more in demand as clients have to buy more and more drugs. On the other hand, the cost to the individual user will only increase, whereas the effects from the use of greater amounts will remain much as before. Increased drug use drives many users to steal, borrow or beg what they need, while countless others will turn to prostitution or other serious forms of crime to feed habits. The habits of some users can reach and even, in extreme cases, exceed £200 per day. Even heavy cannabis users can find themselves needing as much as £150 per week. Many drug users will be forced to sell possessions to which they may be very attached, only realising a fraction of their true value, in order to fund their habit.

Addiction

Drug users may become physically or psychologically addicted to substances they use. If use of the preferred drug is stopped or reduced once a tolerance has built, due to non-availability or expense, then users will begin to feel unpleasant symptoms of physical or psychological withdrawal. These may lead to great pain or discomfort and sufferers may feel that they cannot carry on with their normal day-to-day lives without use of the drug. Many heavy users of drugs no longer get any positive feelings from the drugs that they use, but may simply take them to feel 'normal'. Many drug addicts will then turn to injecting drugs to achieve greater effects.

Withdrawal

Withdrawal symptoms from drug use can range from slight discomfort to life-threatening situations, depending on the drug or drugs being used, their strength and purity, the quantities used and the regularity of use. Withdrawal symptoms are common with illegal drugs and some legal drugs too, such as alcohol (hangover), nicotine (cravings and mood changes) and even coffee (anxiety). In certain circumstances withdrawal symptoms can necessitate hospitalisation. Medical supervision, advice and intervention is recommended for all serious situations. Abrupt withdrawal from some drugs, such as heroin or even tranquillisers, can lead to serious and distressing symptoms.

Health

All substances that are taken into the body, whether by mouth, injection, smoking or sniffing, eventually find their way to the brain via the bloodstream. They will be filtered and processed by the lungs, stomach, liver and kidneys. Apart from the fact that brain cells may be killed off (e.g. with alcohol or ecstasy use), use of drugs cause many other health-related problems, as follows:

- **Heroin** – overdose (due to depressant effect), physical addiction, withdrawal symptoms, HIV, hepatitis, gangrene, collapsed veins, septicaemia, abscesses due to injecting, nausea and vomiting, severe constipation and weakening of the immune system.

- **Amphetamine (speed)** – mental illness, psychosis, paranoia, depression, anxiety, immune system damage leading to other illnesses, hyperthermia (overheating), insomnia, suppression of appetite, diarrhoea and raising of blood pressure leading to an increased risk of strokes.

- **Ecstasy** – blood clots, hyperthermia, confusion, lockjaw, dehydration, kidney and liver cancer, raising of blood pressure leading to an increased risk of strokes, convulsions, nausea and vomiting, brain damage, personality disorders and mood swings.

- **Cannabis** – short-term memory loss, loss of co-ordination, cancers of tongue, lips, throat, mouth and lungs, bronchitis, impotency, psychosis, paranoia, schizophrenia, panic attacks and anxiety.

- **Alcohol** – cirrhosis of liver, death of brain cells, loss of coordination, raised blood pressure, death if used with certain other depressant drugs, mental illnesses, personality disorders.

- **Injecting** – Hepatitis B or C virus which could lead to serious or fatal health problems in later life, HIV, gangrene, collapsed veins, septicaemia, abscesses and skin ulcers.

- **Adulterants** – the majority of street drugs are also 'cut' or adulterated with other substances that are potentially harmful, especially if injected. It is quite common for substances to be sold that are not what they claim to be at all. These are known as 'snidey' drugs and can contain all sorts of dangerous substances.

Illegality

The majority of street drugs are illegal substances and the possession of them can lead to a court conviction and a prison sentence. Manufacture or supply of an illegal drug can attract even greater sentences and the offender's assets may also be seized. In law the offence of 'supply' is complete if a person simply passes a 'joint' or 'spliff' to another person for him or her to take a draw from. No money needs to change hands.

Once a person has a drugs conviction it can stay with him or her for life and cause all sorts of problems, such as restrictions in career choices and travel opportunities. Many professions and businesses will not take on a person with a drugs conviction, and many countries throughout the world will not grant entry visas to the person for the same reason.

It is not true that the police only caution for possession of drugs nowadays; it depends upon many other circumstances, such as class of drug, amount, etc. Drugs are classified into three groups depending on how dangerous they are considered to be:

class A – heroin, cocaine, crack, ecstasy, LSD

class B – amphetamine

class C – cannabis, many prescription tranquillisers and hypnotics.

For penalties, see Worksheet 17.2.

Follow-up exercises

The exercise can be supported and reinforced by the distribution to participants of drug information literature for them to study in their own time.

17.1 Six Things to Consider if You are Using or Thinking of Using Drugs

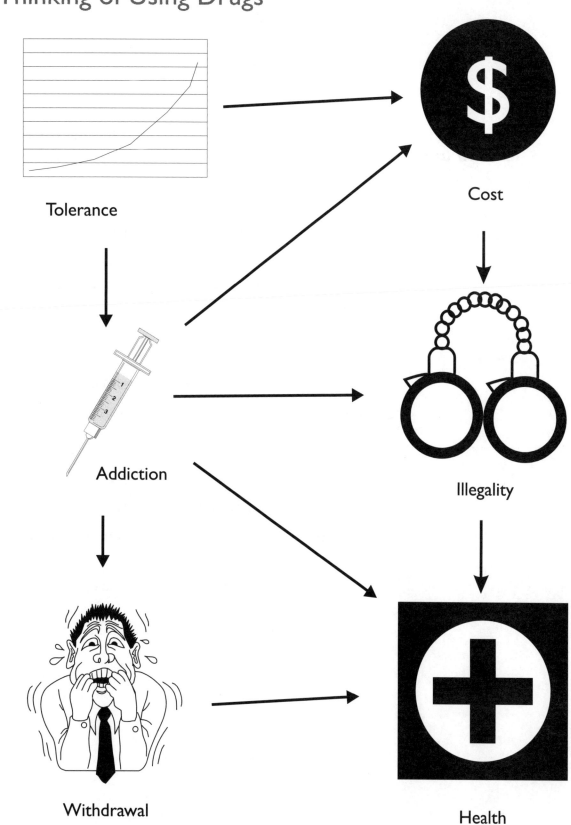

Tolerance

Cost

Addiction

Illegality

Withdrawal

Health

17.2 Maximum penalties

	Possession for own use	Possession with intent to supply	Supply	Manufacture or cultivation
A	7 years	Life Unlimited fine Seizure of assets	Life Unlimited fine Seizure of assets	Life Unlimited fine Seizure of assets
B	5 years	14 years Unlimited fine Seizure of assets	14 years Unlimited fine Seizure of assets	14 years Unlimited fine Seizure of assets
C	2 years	5 years Unlimited fine Seizure of assets	5 years Unlimited fine Seizure of assets	5 years Unlimited fine Seizure of assets

An Unnecessary Death

Suggested age: 13+ • Suggested length of exercise: 1 hour for each exercise

Outline

An exercise that can be used as a stimulus for discussion work, role play and writing. It allows participants to explore several aspects that surround the accidental death of a young person who is under the influence of lighter fuel gas and the actions of his friends.

Purpose and expected outcome

- To encourage participants to consider the possible results of substance use in dangerous circumstances.

- To allow participants to examine the responsibilities of a drug user's friends.

- To enable participants to consider the wider consequences of individual drug use.

- To challenge attitudes to drug use.

- To reinforce drug prevention messages.

Method

Using the story sheet (18.1) as a stimulus, the class can be set all or some of the following tasks.

Task one

Write a dramatic essay about the accident and the circumstances leading up to it. You may invent any fact or other characters that you wish to include but must not change any of the given facts. Make the essay as dramatic as possible.

Task two

Working in pairs, one person takes the part of a police officer and the other person the part of a witness to the accident. The police officer is to interview the witness about what they saw and prepare a written statement based on that interview. The pair can then swap round so that they change roles. A specimen police statement form is included for this task (18.2).

Task three

Such an accident would certainly make the front page of your local newspaper. Reproduce that front page, including the masthead, headline and feature story, together with any other extras that might be found on the front page of your local newspaper. The story should be written in a journalistic style and include at least one short quote from a witness.

Task four

Write a letter to your local newspaper expressing your views about the accident. The letter is for publication and should be powerful and to the point.

Task five

Write a letter from one of the group to John's parents. The letter should express how sorry you are about what happened. The letter need not be overlong but should express in a clear way exactly how you feel.

Role plays

The story can also be used as a stimulus for individuals or groups to role play some or all of the following situations:

1. The conversation between John and the rest of the group when he suggests to them that they should buy some gas and use it by the railway line.

2. The decision of Paul and Liza not to use gas on that day and the reaction of the rest of the group to that decision.

3. The time that Helen and John told the rest of the group about their use of amphetamine and the reaction of the rest of the group to the information.

4. The actions of Paul and Liza while the other members of the group are sniffing, and their conversations.

5. The moment when Jason reaches John's dead body just after it has been struck by the train.

6. The moment when the train driver reaches the body after bringing the train to an emergency stop.

7. The rest of the group's reaction to the accident in the first few minutes following the collision.

8. The arrival of the police and their conversations with the group members.

9. The arrival of the police at John's home and their conversation with his parents, telling them of the accident.

10. The moment when John's parents tell his brothers and sisters about the accident, and their reactions to the news.

11. A conversation between John's mother and the rest of the group some days after the accident, during which she blames them for what happened.

12. A conversation between the train driver and other rail workers concerning nightmares about seeing John right in front of the train cab just before the impact.

13. A conversation between the surviving members of the group after attending John's funeral.

14. A conversation between John's parents following the funeral.

15. An assembly given by the head teacher of John's school, telling the rest of the school about the accident at the start of the new term. This will include the head teacher's thoughts about the responsibilities of all concerned.

Notes for teacher or group leader

The written part of this exercise can form the basis of a number of lessons, spaced out over several weeks. The role-play part of the exercise can be carried out in small groups or using the whole class. The whole story can be used as a basis for a complete dramatic play about the incident which could then be performed in front of the whole school or indeed taken to other schools in the area.

Follow-up exercises

An accidental death of this nature would be the subject of a legal inquest of some sort. The story could be used as the basis for a mock inquest into all of the circumstances surrounding the accident. At such an inquest each member of the group would be required to attend and give evidence along with anyone else involved in the accident, during which they would be questioned by lawyers representing the rail authorities and by the coroner.

18.1 An Unnecessary Death (1)

The main railway line ran in a shallow cutting along the back of the allotments near to the Manor's Field housing estate. The time was 11.45 am on Monday 15 August. Five youths, John Weston, Jason Fielding, Liza Williams, Paul Shields and Helen Roberts, all aged 14 years, were sitting at the foot of the embankment close to the line.

The group were on holiday from school and this was a favourite place for them to meet. The railway line was fenced off, but a part of the fence had been broken down earlier that summer and the group had no difficulty in getting through. They liked the place because it was out of sight of anyone working on the allotments.

They occupied their time exploring the copse at the edge of the line and messing about in the small work huts that lay close to the line. Trains passed about every 20 minutes, and the group had hidden from them at first because they feared that the driver would report them to the police for trespassing. After the first few times they had got fed up with hiding and now didn't bother as to whether they were seen or not.

On this particular day the group moved into one of the work huts, some of them sniffing lighter fuel gas from refill canisters. The group had tried gas several times before, and all had smoked cannabis on lots of occasions. John and Helen had told the others that they had also tried amphetamine and ecstasy. That day it had been John's idea to buy some cans of gas from one of the local shops and to use them by the railway line. Liza and Paul had decided not to sniff on that day but the others used the gas for a few minutes and, with the exception of Helen, were all shouting and laughing and getting very high. Helen had been very sick and had passed out on the floor in the corner of the hut.

John did not like the sight or smell of the vomit and staggered outside. He sat for a few minutes until his can of gas was empty, and then he began to pick up stones from the side of the line. At first he just threw the stones randomly all around him but then he began to throw them through the smashed windows of the hut at the rest of the group. He was laughing hysterically as he did so and fell over several times.

18.1 An Unnecessary Death (2)

One of the stones hit Jason on the forehead, after bouncing off an inside wall, and made a deep cut. Jason got very angry and ran out of the hut screaming and shouting at the top of his voice. He was completely out of control and picked up a heavy piece of metal. John laughed at him and threw another stone. This missed and Jason chased John along the edge of the track.

They had only gone a few yards when Jason was passed by a fast-moving Intercity train travelling along the line nearest to him. John had his back to the train and was so high on the gas that he didn't hear it coming. He turned to run across the tracks and was struck by the train. The impact threw him halfway up the embankment. He suffered massive injuries all over his body and died instantly.

✓

18.2 Witness Statement Form

Statement of: _____

Over 21 ☐   Under 21 ☐   Age if under 21:

This statement is true to the best of my knowledge and belief and I make it knowing that, if it is tendered in evidence, I shall be liable to prosecution if I have wilfully stated in it anything which I know to be false or do not believe to be true.

Date: _____ day of _____ 20 _____

Signature: _____

Signature witnessed by: _____

Useful Organisations

UK

Alcoholics Anonymous
HQ, PO Box 1, Stonebow House, Stonebow, York YO1 7NJ
Tel: 01904 644026 (For local branches consult your telephone directory.)
Website: www.alcoholics-anonymous.org.uk

Childline Helpline
0800 11 11 (Free, confidential, 24-hour helpline for children in trouble or danger.)
Website: www.childline.org.uk

Citizens Advice Bureau
For local branches consult your telephone directory.

Cynulliad Cenedlaethol Cymru (National Assembly for Wales)
Website: www.wales.org.uk/subisocialpolicy/topics-e.htm#misuse
Details of drug services in Wales.

DrugScope
Formed by the amalgamation of ISDD and SCODA.
Provides expert information, training and resources.
32–36 Loman Street, London SE1 0EE
Tel: 020 7928 1211
Website: www.drugscope.org.uk

Narcotics Anonymous
UK Service Office, 202 City Road, London EC1V 2PH
National help line 020 7730 0009 (10am to 10pm daily)
Email: ukso@ukna.org
Website: www.ukna.org (gives details of international contacts)

National AIDs Helpline
Tel: 0800 567 123 (24-hour advice and counselling service)

National Drugs Helpline
Tel: 0800 77 66 00 (Free, confidential 24-hour service for users, their families and friends)
Website: www.patient.co.uk
Website designed for young people: www.talktofrank.com

Northern Ireland Council for Voluntary Action
61 Duncairn Gardens, Belfast BT15 2GB
Tel: 028 9087 7777
Website: www.nicva.org
Details of drug services in Northern Ireland.

Parentline Plus
UK registered charity that offers support to anyone parenting a child.
Free help line: 0808 800 2222
Website: www.parentlineplus.org.uk

Rape Crisis
Provides counselling, advice and support to survivors of rape or sexual assault.
Website: www.rapecrisis.org.uk/helplinenumbers.htm (gives contact details of local services)

Release
388 Old Street London EC1V 9LT
Administration tel: 020 7729 5255
Helpline: 0845 4500 215 (24-hour advice, information and referral on legal and drug-related problems for users, their families and friends.)
Website: www.release.org.uk

Re-Solv
30a High Street, Stone, Staffordshire ST15 8AW
Tel: 01785 817885
Help line 0808 800 2345 (Free, confidential 24-hour service to users, their families and friends)
Website: www.re-solv.org
Works to reduce and prevent solvent abuse.

Samaritans

National lo-call number 08457 90 90 90 (For local branches consult your telephone directory)

Website: www.samaritans.org.uk

Scottish Drugs Forum

Shaftesbury House, 5 Waterloo Street, Glasgow G2 6AY

Tel: 0141 221 1175

Website: www.sdf.org.uk

Details of drug services in Scotland.

Australia

National Drugs Strategy Committee

GPO Box 9848, Canberra, ACT2601

Tel: 6 289 7731

Fax: 6 282 5430

Drugs education website: www.dest.gov.au/schools/drugeducation/NSDES.htm

Canada

Canadian Centre on Substance Abuse/National Clearing House on Substance Abuse

112 Kent Street, S

ite 480, Ottawa KIP 5P2

Tel: 613 235 4048

Information and advice concerning substance abuse.

Website: www.ccsa.ca

Ireland

The Department of Health

Hawkins House, Dublin 2, Republic of Ireland

Provides details of services available.

Website: www.tcd.ie/community_health

The Netherlands

Netherlands Institute of Mental Health and Addiction

PO Box, 725 3500 AS Utrecht

Tel: 030 297 11 00 Fax: 030 297 11 11

Provides advice and literature on drug matters.

Website: www.trimbos.nl/defaults37.html

New Zealand

National Society on Alcohol and Drug Dependence (NSAD)

20 Paramoana Street, Ponrua

Tel: 4 237 0273

Provides advice and literature on drug matters.

Website: www.nsad.org.nz

New Zealand Drug Foundation

PO Box 3082, Wellington

Tel: 4 499 2920 Fax: 4 499 2925

Provides advice and literature on drug matters.

Website: www.nzdf.org.nz

USA

National Clearinghouse for Alcohol and Drug Information

PO Box 2345, Rockville, MD 20852

Information and advice concerning substance abuse.

Website: www.health.org

Cocaine Helpline

Tel: 800 C.O.C.A.I.N.E.

24-hour free and confidential help regarding cocaine use.

National Institute on Drug

Abuse Hotline: 1 800 662 H.E.L.P. 24-hour free and confidential help and referral for people with drug problems.

Provides advice and literature on drug matters.

Website: www.nida.nih.gov

For details of other voluntary and statutory agencies in your area that may be able to offer help, advice or information, look in your local telephone directory under 'Help and advice'.